Praise for Joe Friel & *Your First Triathlon*

"Twenty-five years of active multisport coaching has proven that Joe Friel has an unprecedented understanding of endurance sports. As a multiple triathlon world champion, I would consider Joe as one of the leading figures in triathlon coaching today. Joe's professional approach and practical understanding of sports physiology has helped many endurance athletes of all abilities reach their full athletic potential."

—SIMON LESSING, 5-TIME TRIATHLON WORLD CHAMPION

"With *Your First Triathlon*, Joe Friel uses his expert knowledge to help new triathletes use the same training principles that have made the *Triathlete's Training Bible* such a success."

—GALE BERNHARDT, USA TRIATHLON OLYMPIC COACH

"Joe does the hard work for the beginning triathlete by condensing, prioritizing, and simplifying all the science and practical experience, which he has mastered over decades of coaching."

—BARB LINDQUIST, 2004 USA OLYMPIC TEAM

"Joe Friel has made me a stronger, healthier, and faster triathlete."

—RALPH HEATH, AGE-GROUP TRIATHLETE

"I'm a mom and an anchorwoman, and thanks to Joe's amazing coaching plan, an Ironman Hawaii Triathlete after only 5 months of training!"

—MARTY VELASCO HAMES, KTVD, PHOENIX, AZ

"Whether you're a beginning triathlete or a seasoned pro, Joe Friel is the leading authority on triathlon training."

—RYAN BOLTON, 2000 USA OLYMPIC TEAM AND IRONMAN WINNER

"Joe Friel's wealth of knowledge in triathlon is astounding, and he has a wonderful way of sharing that knowledge with all athletes: beginners to elite professionals. If you are looking to get off to a great start in this sport, you have come to the right place!"

—SIRI LINDLEY, TRIATHLON WORLD CHAMPION

YOUR FIRST TRIATHLON

YOUR FIRST TRIATHLON

Joe Friel

BOULDER • COLORADO

VeloPress®
1830 55th Street
Boulder, Colorado 80301–2700 USA
(303) 440-0601; Fax: (303) 444-6788; E-mail: velopress@competitorgroup.com

To purchase additional copies of this book or other VeloPress books, call (800) 811-4210, ext. 2169, or visit www.velopress.com.

Distributed in the United States and Canada by Ingram Publisher Services.

Cover and interior design by Erin Johnson
Illustrations by Todd Telander
Cover photos by Don Karle; Brad Kaminski (goggles)

Library of Congress Cataloging-in-Publication Data
Friel, Joe.
  Your first triathlon / Joe Friel.
    p. cm.
  Includes index.
  ISBN: 978-1-931382-85-4 (pbk. : alk. paper)
  1. Triathlon—Training—Handbooks, manuals, etc. I. Title.
GV1060.73.F75 2006
796.42'57—dc22
                                                                    2005031430

This book is printed on 100 percent recovered/recycled fiber, 30 percent postconsumer waste, elemental chlorine free, using soy-based inks.

Printed in the United States of America.
10 9

CONTENTS

To "Sunshine"—my granddaughter, Keara Friel,
who is training for her first triathlon.
Keara is 3 years old.

ACKNOWLEDGMENTS

I WANT TO THANK THE THOUSANDS of triathletes I have coached, consulted with, spoken to, and answered questions for over the past twenty-five years. They have provided the passion of triathlon. I also want to thank the many coaches with whom I have worked closely since the time, nearly twenty years ago, when I found out about the *other* triathlon coach in the United States, to now, when there are hundreds. They have provided the understanding of triathlon.

I especially want to thank Bob Hinkel, who owns and operates the LaCamas Swim and Sport Club in Camas, Washington, and every year enlists, encourages, and assists a group of triathletes preparing for their first races at various distances. The idea for this book came to me over dinner with Bob in February 2005.

INTRODUCTION

WELCOME TO THE SPORT OF TRIATHLON!

You're about to embark on an exciting adventure that will improve your fitness, boost your health, and raise your self-esteem. Most of all, it will make your life richer and more enjoyable. While triathlon is fun, it is also challenging. In fact, it may well be the challenge that attracted you. Most new triathletes tell me they came to the sport simply to see if they could do it—to challenge themselves. Once they tried it, they were hooked.

I'm sure that mastering three endurance sports and doing them all back-to-back, nonstop, seems like a rather daunting task. It should, but I'm sure you can do it. I've helped many people become triathletes over the past twenty-five years. With your motivation and my guidance, I'm certain you will do just fine. I have no doubt that, armed with the answers to basic questions and a dedication to training, you will successfully finish your first triathlon in a few weeks. That is the single purpose of this book—for you to cross the finish line with a smile on your face and become a triathlete.

Your First Triathlon provides the answers to many common triathlon questions:

- How do I need to train?
- What should I eat?
- Do I need a new bike?
- Which race should I enter?
- Should I buy special triathlon clothing?
- What happens at a triathlon?

Of course, there are hundreds of other questions you will have before your first race. Due to its inherent nature, blending three sports into one, triathlon is a complex undertaking. Most of your questions will be answered in the following pages, but there could be some left unresolved after you've read this book. Another resource you can use is my Web site, www.yourfirsttri.com. There you will find a list of frequently asked questions. Believe me, if you have a question, someone else has had that same question before, and we can help you with it.

Your First Triathlon gently guides you through the adventure of preparing for a sprint-distance triathlon. In the first four chapters the basics of getting your lifestyle organized around triathlon training are discussed. This includes such topics as understanding the basics of the sport, setting goals, controlling body weight, eating for triathlon, and outside support.

Chapters 5 through 8 cover the nuts and bolts of triathlon training—swimming, biking, and running. Here you'll also find simple ways to improve muscle strength and flexibility to avoid injuries and become more fit. Then we bring it all together in Chapter 9 with a training plan that fits your new lifestyle and your level of commitment. If you've just discovered this book and have your first triathlon coming up in twelve weeks or less, start with Chapter 9 so you can begin training right away. Then go back and read the supporting chapters.

Chapter 10 is a quick overview of the high-tech equipment you may want to buy to train more effectively. And finally, Chapter 11 gets you ready to go to your first triathlon feeling confident. Here you'll discover how to choose the right race for you, what to expect on race day and before, how to dress, what exactly you need to bring with you, how to set up a transition, and what to expect when finishing the race.

The appendixes provide you with more helpful information, including lists of novice-friendly races, Web and book resources, checklists, and a glossary of triathlon terms. Whenever you come across a term you don't understand, check out Appendix A "Triathlon Lingo." Appendixes B through F provide the details you need to do the workouts listed in Chapter 9.

All of this probably seems a bit overwhelming. That's understandable; the sport of triathlon can be quite intimidating at first. But learning in small doses what to expect and what it takes to get there will make this challenge less daunting and more fun. And fun is what it's all about. Let's get started!

Chapter 1

YOUR NEW CHALLENGE

Why do you want to do a triathlon? Maybe it's because you've heard that exercise is good for you and that people who exercise regularly have a lower risk of heart disease, cancer, and other diseases, that they live longer and have a better quality of life. Or maybe it's because exercise has been shown to reduce stress, promote clear thinking and creativity, and build confidence.

Although these are all good reasons to do a triathlon, I'll bet it's none of these. Chances are you are doing a triathlon because a friend is entered and has talked you into doing it also. Or it could be that you need a new challenge in your life, and triathlon looks like a sport that will test your limits. There's no doubt that it will. Or possibly losing weight, looking better, and eating without guilt motivates you. Then again, maybe you just want to have fun. These are all good reasons. Triathlon can help you accomplish all of these goals and more.

YOUR TRI GOAL

Regardless of your reason, you certainly want your first triathlon to go well, so you bought this book to find tips on preparing. You did the right thing. I've been coaching triathletes since the early days of the sport and have prepared many novices for their first races. I'm sure I can help you, too. This book is filled with triathlon tips to guide you from just starting to train to crossing the finish line.

Let's start with the most basic tip—setting a goal for your first triathlon. I've been telling new triathletes this for more than twenty-five years: You should have only one goal for your first triathlon—to finish the race with a smile on your face.

1

It doesn't matter what your time is or how you place in your age group or even if you are one of the last finishers. Just finish the race. Nothing else matters, other than the smile, of course. Those who follow this advice have a lot of fun and a long triathlon career. Those who disregard it almost always finish their first triathlon depressed and don't stay in the sport for very long. My purpose in this book is to help you accomplish this simple goal. I will be coaching you, and I'm certain that if you follow what I have written in the following pages, you will be successful.

HISTORY

Triathlon got its start in Southern California in 1974, when the San Diego Track Club added a short race to its calendar, a combination of running 4.8 miles, biking 5 miles, and swimming half a mile. In 1978 the first Ironman triathlon was held in Oahu, Hawaii, with fifteen participants. The race was meant to determine who was the best athlete—the swimmer, the biker, or the runner. The athletes swam 2.4 miles at Waikiki Beach, biked 115 miles around the island, and ran a 26.2-mile marathon. The first winner, Gordon Haller, was a former navy pentathlete.

For the next twenty years the sport grew slowly but steadily, with a mix of both short- and long-distance races. In 1996 the International Olympic Committee announced that triathlon would be an Olympic sport in the 2000 Games in Sydney, Australia, a country that had also embraced triathlon. At the Sydney Olympics the women's triathlon was the first event, with the men's race the following day. Both were televised around the world and created a lot of interest in the sport. Since then triathlon has experienced phenomenal growth both in the United States and abroad.

RACE DISTANCES

Today there are four common triathlon distances. The longest, and the one most people think of when they hear the word "triathlon," is the Ironman-distance or "ultra-distance" race. Ironman is the most readily recognized race, probably because it gets the most press and has been around a long time. The swim is 4,000 meters in open water, the bike portion is 112 miles, and the run is 26.2 miles. The winning time is generally between eight and nine hours, and the last-finisher cutoff time is usually seventeen hours.

The next distance is the half-Ironman or "long-course" race, with a 2,000-meter open-water swim, 56-mile bike ride, and 13.1-mile run. This is a very popular distance with seasoned triathletes and is growing rapidly. The participants complete the race in about four to eight hours.

The Olympic-distance triathlon, sometimes called the "international-distance" race, goes back to the early 1980s and is the distance used in Olympic and World Cup competition. In these elite-only events the athletes are allowed to draft, or follow closely behind each other, on the bike. In almost all of the races done by amateurs, regardless of distance, drafting is not allowed. The Olympic-distance swim is 1,500 meters, the bike leg is 25 miles, and the run is 6.2 miles. The pros generally complete the race in under two hours, with the last finishers taking four to five hours.

The shortest-distance triathlon is called the "sprint" or "short-course" race. The typical sprint is a half-mile swim, 13-mile bike ride, and 3-mile run. The swim is often done in a pool, which makes it a good event for the triathlon newbie. Open water can be a bit intimidating to the novice swimmer. These races take one to two hours to complete, so they are hardly a real "sprint," except when compared with an Ironman.

The typical sprint is a half-mile swim, 13-mile bike ride, and 3-mile run. The swim is often done in a pool, which makes it a good event for the triathlon newbie. Open water can be a bit intimidating to the novice swimmer.

You'll find there are slight variations in these distances and that there are some that don't fit neatly into any of these categories. There are also other combinations of the three sports, such as swim-run-bike and run-bike-swim. Run-bike-run races are called "duathlons" or sometimes "biathlons." Some cities have swim-run races, known officially by the tongue-twisting name "aquathlon," but usually called something like "splash and dash" or "stroke and stride." The distances for these sport variations are not standard, but they tend to be like the Olympic- or sprint-distance triathlons.

YOUR FIRST RACE

If you have decided on a race to enter, I hope it is a sprint-distance triathlon. There is currently a disturbing trend in triathlon for newcomers to take on the Ironman-distance race as their first. They apparently want to experience the ultimate challenge right away. Most have no idea what they are doing and are in for a rude awakening. Not only is the difficulty of completing the event on race day beyond what most could even imagine, training for such an endeavor is like taking a part-time job.

The best way to prepare for an Ironman-distance triathlon is to start by doing a sprint and then work your way up to it by completing several Olympic races and a few half-Ironman distances. Starting with an Ironman can be devastating and generally leads to a very short tri career.

How much time does it take to train for a sprint? You can do it in less than five hours a week if you follow the training plan in Chapter 9. With a day off each week to make sure you get enough rest, that works out to less than an hour a day. Of course, if you have more time than that you can do more workouts. The training plan allows for that by including optional swim, bike, and run workouts each week.

THE NEWBIE

In the early days of the sport (ca. 1983), most of those doing a first triathlon were injured runners. That's how I got started. Every time I'd break down while training for the next marathon, I'd get my bike out of the garage and ride it. Then one day I had a bad bike accident and broke my shoulder. The doctor said one of the best ways to rehabilitate it was swimming. While in the pool one day after the shoulder had healed, it dawned on me that I was swimming, biking, and running, so why not try out that new sport—triathlon. I did and was hooked.

Things have changed since then. Most people who are new to triathlon don't have a background in another sport. For them triathlon is their first and only sport. Part of the attraction of triathlon for newcomers is that it's a bit like being a kid again, with lots of variety and options. It's fun to alternate swimming, biking, and running instead of being stuck with one sport. What better way to seek a brief escape from the daily chores and responsibilities of life than to head to the pool or go out on the road?

Most outside observers see triathletes as masochists and can't imagine why anyone would want to do this. That's probably due to the sport's roots and Julie Moss's famous crawl to the finish line in the Hawaii Ironman® in 1982. The media still foster this image of the "gruelathon," of participants "pushing the limits of human endurance" and fighting through unbelievable suffering as they struggle to the finish. It really isn't like that, but don't get me wrong—triathlon is hard work. You won't get fit in three sports without dedication and perseverance. Although you've probably done harder things, this will rank right up there with some of the bigger challenges of your life. But it will also be one of the most fun challenges you've ever taken on.

CAN YOU DO IT?

Attitude in sport is everything. If you believe in yourself and reinforce positive thinking habits daily, you will succeed. Your goal is to finish a triathlon. I know you can do it because I've seen many others succeed. In fact, I've never had anyone fail who followed the guidelines and training program I present here. I believe in you.

Others also believe you can do it. But there may be some who don't and may even have told you so. The most important opinion, however, is yours.

Do you believe? What is the voice in your head saying about your chances of success as a triathlete? When it comes to success or failure in this sport, the voice in your head can be your strongest ally or your greatest enemy. You decide which it will be.

If you've trained the voice to find fault, you probably won't make it across that finish line. But if your self talk is positive, success is practically assured. Negative self talk focuses your mind on the obstacles. And your mind will come up with plenty of obstacles to get you out of training: "I'm too busy to work out today." "I'm too tired to get up early." "I just don't feel like it." A positive attitude allows you to clearly see ways around such obstacles and keeps you on track.

Certainly there will be setbacks; that's the way life is. Instead of dwelling on what you could have done, look instead for the learning experience in every misfortune. The only difference between winning and losing in triathlon, as in life, is that when we fail, we learn something—or at least we should.

Imagine how boring and unfulfilling life would be without obstacles. Where would the thrill of victory come from if there wasn't an agony of defeat? Obstacles are good. Accept them while focusing on their challenges, and you will enjoy satisfaction and fulfillment in triathlon and life. Wallow in them, and you ensure defeat. Some opposition is always necessary for attainment. Kites rise against, not with, the wind.

Defeat in whatever form is often blamed on physical obstacles, such as lack of some physical ability, like endurance, strength, or speed. The negative thinker sees this obstacle as insurmountable. The positive athlete instead sees two opportunities: taking advantage of known strengths and learning about weaknesses so they can be improved upon. Endurance, strength, and speed can all be developed.

What if you don't see the opportunities? First, recognition of your shortcomings and willingness to change are 90 percent of developing a positive attitude. The final 10 percent comes with positive reinforcement, practiced daily. Here's a strategy that will help. Every night when you go to bed, between the time when the lights go out and you fall asleep, review your greatest success of the day, no matter how trivial. Perhaps you completed a workout that was difficult; relive that accomplishment. It could even be something as seemingly minor as starting a workout when motivation was low. Mentally celebrate the victory. Remember your successes every day, and your attitude and belief in yourself will soon improve.

Chapter 2

YOUR TRIATHLON LIFESTYLE

Preparing for your first triathlon will demand a lot of you. First and foremost, it requires dedication. You can't successfully train for a triathlon if you aren't dedicated to exercise. You must go through each and every day with exercise as a focal point. Everything you do and when you do it must be determined by your next workout. This includes eating, working, mowing the lawn, preparing meals, hobbies, and all other interests. The successful triathlete decides when the next workout will be and then arranges the other details of life around it.

This may sound obsessive, and I suppose it is to some extent. But one person's passion is another's obsession. If you want to finish your first triathlon in a few weeks, you will need some measure of obsession (or passion) for exercise and a healthy lifestyle. If you don't enjoy swimming, biking, and running, chances are that you will never make it to the start line, let alone to the finish line.

LIFE AS A TRIATHLETE

How are you going to fit swimming, biking, and running into your already busy life? The goal of finishing a sprint triathlon is a worthy one, but the reality is that your free time is quite limited. It won't be easy at first; you'll miss some workouts due to other commitments. On those days you will question whether you can really get in shape for a triathlon.

Despite the inevitable setbacks, there is no doubt that you can do it if you fully commit to your goal. You must also accept that you are not perfect, and there will be days when things don't go right. Even experienced triathletes miss workouts due to other important responsibilities. However, missing a workout must be a rare occurrence rather than a common one if you are to become a triathlete. Consistency is key to success.

Several other things will lead to your triathlon success, including your level of motivation, recovery from exercise, staying healthy, eating nutritious food, controlling body weight, the help and support you receive, and even how you age. In this chapter we look at all of these factors except nutrition, which is the subject of Chapter 3, and your support system, which is discussed in Chapter 4.

MOTIVATION

There will be times when you ask yourself, "Why am I doing this?" While most people are sleeping in on Saturday morning, you'll be working out. Unlike your coworkers who go home after work to drink a beer and watch TV, you'll head home to get your run in before dinner.

Success in triathlon depends heavily on motivation. It's easy to say you're going to train for a triathlon; it's another thing entirely to drive to the pool at 5:30 A.M. or hop on your bike right after work when it was a tough day. It's not always easy to incorporate a self-improvement program into an already busy life. More than half of those who start an exercise program quit within a few weeks. What can you do to make it through the weeks leading up to your first triathlon?

Staying the Course

The starting point is to follow the training plan laid out in Chapter 9. This eliminates one stumbling block—deciding what to do each day. Just follow the plan. There will be days when you miss a workout; that happens to all triathletes. But you must see this as the exception rather than the rule. You also must not be too hard on yourself if this happens. If you find yourself looking for reasons not

⊙ SHOULD YOU GET A PHYSICAL?

Should you see your doctor for a complete physical before starting a triathlon training program? The following questions about your health are suggested by the American College of Sports Medicine (ACSM), to help you decide. If you answer "Yes" to one or more of these questions, the ACSM recommends that you see your doctor before starting an exercise program or increasing your current level of exercise.

Self-Screening Questions

__ Yes __ No   1. Has your doctor ever told you that you have a heart condition?

__ Yes __ No   2. Do you feel pain in your chest when you do physical activity?

__ Yes __ No   3. Did you or do you now have a heart murmur that a physician considered significant?

__ Yes __ No   4. In the past month, have you had chest pain when you were not doing physical activity?

__ Yes __ No   5. Have you ever had pain, pressure, or a squeezing feeling in your chest that came on during exercise or other physical activity?

__ Yes __ No   6. Do you lose balance because of dizziness or do you ever lose consciousness?

__ Yes __ No   7. If you climb a few flights of stairs fairly rapidly, do you have tightness or a pressing pain in your chest?

__ Yes __ No   8. Have you ever experienced problems breathing while exercising?

__ Yes __ No   9. Do you have a bone or joint problem that could be made worse by a change in your physical activity?

__ Yes __ No   10. Is your doctor currently prescribing drugs (for example, water pills) for your blood pressure or a heart condition?

__ Yes __ No   11. Do you know of any other reason why you should not participate in a physical activity?

__ Yes __ No   12. Has it been longer than twelve months since your last physical?

to work out, however, it may be time for a gut check. You may need to consider a few things to maintain motivation.

Remind yourself why you want to do a triathlon. Recall every day the benefits of tri training, including keeping your weight and blood pressure down, strengthening your heart and muscles, improving your flexibility, building greater stamina, and feeling good about yourself. Envision what it will be like when you cross that finish line on race day, having achieved a major goal in your life. Do this mental drill whenever you see your resolve flagging.

Sometimes it helps to visualize the effects of *not* continuing to work out regularly: further loss of fitness, possible weight gain, increasingly weak and inflexible muscles, more rapid aging, and a greater risk for heart disease and cancer. Here are some other strategies that may help you stay on track:

- Exercise first thing in the morning, when there are fewer interruptions.
- Schedule workouts in a weekly calendar the same as you would other appointments.
- Exercise with a friend; peer support (pressure?) encourages participation.
- Lay out exercise clothes and equipment the night before your workout.
- Ride a wind trainer or stationary bike while watching TV or reading.

IT'S OKAY TO STOP SOMETIMES

Here's a helpful strategy that I have known even professional athletes to use. If you just don't feel like exercising, tell yourself you will only do it for five minutes and then stop. This will get you out the door, and once into it you'll probably finish the workout. But if you still don't feel up to it after five minutes, call it quits and head home. It just wasn't your day. Your body is probably trying to tell you something. Be sure to rest well and strengthen your resolve for tomorrow.

Remember that you are forming new habits, and that takes time. Don't be discouraged if you find the triathlon lifestyle doesn't come easily and on some days exercise is the last thing you want to do. At these times you must consciously decide that your goal is important and recommit to achieving it. Overcoming the temptation to avoid exercise will make you a stronger person and, ultimately, a triathlete.

SLEEPING YOUR WAY TO BETTER FITNESS

Sometimes even new triathletes go too far with their passion for the sport. When pressed for time and feeling the need to fit in a workout or other activity, the first thing most triathletes do is cut back on sleep. They get up earlier or go to bed later in order to wedge more into each day. The problem with this way of "creating" time is that it compromises recovery and adaptation. During rest, especially sleep, the body mends and grows stronger. While you're sleeping, a growth hormone is released, producing a more physically fit body. If the time spent snoozing is shortened, it takes longer to recover. This compromises consistency, which is the single most important aspect of training.

Reducing sleep time also means that energy stores aren't fully replenished between workouts, leading to a drop in endurance performance over several days. The body's cells that are routinely damaged by strenuous exercise will take longer to repair, increasing the risk of injury and illness. If the training workload remains high despite decreased sleep time, overtraining becomes a real threat. Mental burnout is also waiting just around the corner for the triathlete who cuts back on sleep.

> **During rest, especially sleep, the body mends and grows stronger. While you're sleeping, a growth hormone is released, producing a more physically fit body. If the time spent snoozing is shortened, it takes longer to recover. This compromises consistency, which is the single most important aspect of training.**

A well-rested triathlete looks forward to the next workout, enjoys training, is powerful, has good endurance, and progressively grows stronger. A tired triathlete realizes none of these benefits. Never underestimate your need for sleep. The average person typically needs seven or eight hours of sleep every day. As a triathlete, you may need more. As you gradually increase the amount of exercise you're doing, stress will increase, as will the need for slumber. And hours of sleep are not the only issue here; quality of sleep is just as important. The quality of your sleep can be improved by:

- Going to bed at a regular time every night.
- Darkening the room in the last hour before bedtime and narrowing your focus by reading or engaging in light conversation.
- Sleeping in a dark, well-ventilated room that is 60 to 64 degrees Fahrenheit.
- Taking a warm bath before bed.
- Progressively contracting and relaxing each muscle group to induce total body relaxation.
- Avoiding stimulants such as coffee and tea in the last several hours before going to bed.
- Restricting alcohol intake, which interferes with sleep patterns, at least a few hours prior to retiring.

If you feel the need to make more time available for training, instead of cutting back on sleep, look for time wasters in your day and replace them. Perhaps the greatest time waster in most of our lives is television. Serious triathletes have one thing in common—they don't watch much TV.

Triathlon training is much more than simply sweating and breathing hard while swimming, biking, and running. Training also depends heavily on adequate rest. By placing as much importance on sleep as on exercise, you will improve your training consistency as the quality of your workouts rises. The result is better fitness and success as a triathlete.

DO YOU NEED TO LOSE WEIGHT?

Today the average American man weighs 191 pounds and the average American woman tips the scales at 164 pounds. Each is carrying in the neighborhood of 25 to 30 pounds of excess body fat. There is little doubt that this unneeded weight has dire consequences for health. Diabetes, heart disease, and other deadly lifestyle diseases have been linked to obesity, which is officially defined as being 30 pounds or more over one's ideal body weight.

Weight and Exercise

Of less importance but certainly related is the impact of excess weight on triathlon performance. It's been estimated that each pound of additional body fat causes a runner to slow by two seconds per mile and requires an additional three watts of power when climbing a hill on a bike. For the novice triathlete who is 25 pounds overweight, this means, in theory, taking 7 to 8 percent longer to finish a race, or about 8 to 10 minutes in a sprint-distance event. In actuality, it probably means more than just a few minutes; a person this much overweight will probably end up walking most of the run portion because his or her aerobic fitness will be inadequate to move that much mass at a running pace.

Do you need to shed a few pounds? If so, you've already taken a giant step in that direction by deciding to do a triathlon. There is considerable research showing that regular exercise helps to control and reduce body fat. Exercise burns between five and twenty calories per minute depending on the type of exercise and its intensity. By exercising several times a week you will be using calories and working your way toward a slimmer body, better triathlon performances, and improved long-term health. The process of losing excess luggage can be accelerated by controlling your eating.

I know you've heard all this before, and if you're like most people, you've been on diets and even tried exercising. You shed some pounds, but they came back with gusto. So why should it work this time?

For one thing, by following through on your goal to become a triathlete, you'll be changing your lifestyle. This won't be another diet. It will be a new way of seeing exercise, food—and yourself. The difference is attitude and commitment. Triathletes as a whole are lean and fit. You can be, too.

Successful Losers

When trying to understand weight loss the place to start is with those who have successfully lost weight and kept it off. In 1993 researchers at Brown University and Miriam Hospital in Providence, Rhode Island, established the National Weight Control Registry to keep track of people who lose at least 30 pounds and keep it off for at least one year. The people listed in the registry lost an average of 70 pounds and kept it off for six years. Several thousand people are listed in the registry and are studied by the researchers.

A great deal has been learned from this research about successful weight loss. For example, nearly 90 percent of those in the registry used a combination of exercise and reduced caloric intake to lose weight. Most of the women in the study relied heavily on walking for exercise. Men were more likely to run and lift weights. They burned, on average, 2,840 calories per week, or about 400 per day, through exercise, with the men's rate a bit higher than the women's. This amounts to about 4 miles of walking or running each day.

Participants reported eating an average of 1,387 calories daily, with men reporting more than women. This number may be low, as other studies have shown that people tend to underestimate their food intake by as much as 20 percent. If that is true here, then these folks may have been taking in closer to 1,664 calories daily.

You may be wondering how they could lose weight if they were burning 400 calories a day through exercise but taking in 1,664. The answer is found in their *resting metabolic rate.*

Calories Out

Resting metabolic rate (RMR) is the amount of energy the body uses to maintain itself while lying down or sitting. RMR is increased by having greater muscle mass, increasing ambient air temperature, being young, having a higher body temperature, experiencing stress, and the presence of certain hormones. Exercise

TABLE 2.1	CALORIES BURNED DURING DAILY ACTIVITIES*	
Intensity	**Examples**	**Calories/Minute**
Light	Computer work, sitting at desk, watching TV	Included in RMR
Moderate	Gardening, standing, house cleaning, shopping	3–6
Heavy	Digging, shoveling snow, climbing stairs	7–9
Extreme	Lifting and carrying heavy loads	10–12

*Use this table to estimate how many calories you burn per minute throughout your daily activities, not including exercise or rest.

TABLE 2.2	CALORIES BURNED DURING EXERCISE*	
Sport	**Calories/Minute**	**Calories/Distance**
Swimming	10	5/25 yards
Biking	10	45/1 mile
Brisk Walking	6	90/1 mile
Running	11	110/1 mile
Vigorous Weight Lifting	8	—

*This table allows you to roughly estimate the calories you burn during exercise. Actual numbers will vary with body size and intensity. These numbers include the RMR calories that are used during exercise.

causes RMR to rise during recovery. This post-exercise "burn" can account for a few hundred calories daily.

RMR usually makes up about 60 to 75 percent of a person's total daily energy expenditure, with the remainder coming from exercise and normal movement at work, school, and home. Interestingly, eating also raises the RMR by as much as 10 percent, because digesting food burns calories.

You can get a rough estimate of your RMR by multiplying your body weight in pounds by 10. A 160-pound person would have an RMR of roughly 1,600 calories per day. To know that person's total daily energy expenditure, we would need to know how much normal activity he or she does in a day plus calories burned during exercise. See Tables 2.1 and 2.2 to estimate your energy expenditure.

By adding RMR calories to daily activity and exercise calories, you can estimate your total daily energy expenditure by using the following equation:

A. RMR calories   _____

B. Calories burned during normal daily activity   _____

C. Calories burned during exercise   _____

Total daily energy expenditure (A + B + C)   _____

▶ EAT LESS OR EXERCISE MORE?

What is the best way for an athlete to lose weight? Unfortunately, few studies of serious athletes have looked at this question.

One group of researchers, however, has examined the issue in an interesting way. They compared eating less to exercising more to see which was more effective in eliminating excess body fat. They had six endurance-trained men create a 1,000-calorie-per-day deficit for seven days by either exercising more while maintaining their caloric intake or eating less while keeping their exercise the same. With 1,000 calories of increased exercise daily—comparable to running an additional 8 miles or so each day—the men averaged 1.67 pounds of weight loss in a week. The subjects eating 1,000 fewer calories each day lost 4.75 pounds on average for the week. So, according to this study, the old adage that "a calorie is a calorie" doesn't hold true. At least in the short term, restricting food intake appears to have a greater return **on the scales** than does increasing training workload. However, the reduced-food-intake group in this study unfortunately lost a greater percentage of muscle mass than did the increased-exercise group. That is an **ineffective** way to lose weight. If the scales show you're lighter, but you have less muscle to create power, the trade-off is not a good one.

How can you reduce calories and yet maintain muscle mass? Unfortunately that question hasn't been answered for athletes, but it has been for sedentary women. Perhaps the conclusions are also applicable to athletes.

Eat Less or Exercise More?

In 1994, Italian researchers had 25 women eat only 800 calories a day for 21 days. Ten ate a relatively high-protein and low-carbohydrate diet. Fifteen ate a low-protein and high-carbohydrate diet. Both were restricted to 20 percent of calories from fat. The two groups lost similar amounts of weight, but there was a significantly greater loss of muscle on the high-carbohydrate, low-protein diet.

It appears that when calories are reduced to lose weight, the protein content of the diet must be kept at near-normal levels. This assumes, of course, that you're eating adequate protein before starting the diet, which many athletes aren't. When you're training hard, a quality source of protein should be included in every meal, especially when you're trying to lose weight.   ⊛

Calories In

Now that you have an idea of how many calories you burn in a day, the key to weight loss is to eat fewer than that daily. This is typically referred to as "calorie counting" and is a critical part of the National Weight Control Registry participants' strategy. Purchase a food and calorie book at your local drugstore or, better yet, use computer software to more easily manage your counting. You can find one designed for athletes at www.yourfirsttri.com.

In order to lose weight, the registry members created a caloric deficit each day of about 500 to 800 calories. In other words, their average total daily energy expenditure was around 2,200 to 2,500 calories, while they ate just 1,700 calories. Theoretically, a 500-calorie daily deficit would result in the loss of one pound a week of body fat. An 800-calorie deficit would do it in just under five days.

I have often found such a rapid rate of weight loss to be counterproductive for athletes because recovery after workouts is compromised, leading to lower-quality exercise and even forced days off. I have had more success with athletes keeping their deficits at 300 to 500 calories daily. At this rate a pound of fat should come off every seven to twelve days, with fewer negative consequences for recovery from daily exercise. Using the lower rate of loss, which is easier to maintain and less of an emotional burden, you would drop 7 pounds during the twelve-week plans in Chapter 9. This amounts to 28 pounds in a year and could do wonders for your health and for triathlon performances in the future.

Daily Eating Strategies

The following are some strategies you can use to keep your calories in less than your calories out:

- **Buy groceries with a plan in mind.** When putting together your grocery shopping list, decide what foods you will eat in the coming week. Do not buy foods that are not on the list. (Chapter 3 will help you with these shopping decisions.)
- **Keep a record of your daily calories in and out.** Software is very helpful for this, but a calorie-counting book and a notebook will work just as well.
- **Eat a lot of high-fiber, low-calorie foods.** Good examples are fibrous fruits and vegetables. These will contribute to a feeling of satisfaction. Avoid low-fiber, high-calorie foods such as refined starches and sugars.
- **Reduce the variety of foods at a meal.** Research reveals that having lots of choices at a meal causes people to eat more by as much as 25 percent. A meal should be no more than three food types. An example of such a meal is a lean protein (fish, shellfish, poultry), a vegetable (other than white), and fruit or berries for dessert.
- **Stop when you're satisfied, not stuffed.** Pay attention to how you feel while eating and stop when you are no longer hungry. Don't "clean your

plate" as you were taught to do as a child. You can enhance your ability to monitor yourself during a meal by slowing down and paying attention to your body's sensations.

- **Choose smaller portions.** You can always add more if necessary, but having excess on your plate encourages continued eating even if you're no longer hungry. This is more difficult to do when eating out, since serving portions are decided for you. Remind yourself when you go to a restaurant that you don't have to eat everything on your plate.
- **Include your favorite, unhealthy foods—sometimes.** Registry participants actually binged at times. About one day a month they consumed a lot of calories. A few even did this weekly by having a food they wouldn't otherwise eat. Occasionally eating a pizza or a bowl of ice cream does not mean you have failed. "Occasionally" is the key word here.
- **Monitor weight daily.** Registry participants weighed themselves daily to stay in touch with how they were doing.
- **Don't skip meals.** Only 4 percent of those in the registry indicated that they skipped meals. Nearly all ate three meals a day.

What If It Isn't Working?

Realize that the extra weight might not melt away at the rate you'd like it to. There will even be those frustrating days—even weeks—when you stay the same weight or regain weight despite continuing to watch what and how much you eat. These "plateaus" can be very frustrating and tempt you to throw in the towel. Don't do it! Hang in there. The body is fickle about how it gives up its precious fat stores. Be patient; this is a long-term project, so don't expect to be leaner every day.

Also, keep in mind that plenty of good is still happening on the inside when you are going through a dietary change combined with regular exercise. For one thing, while you are losing fat you are probably also gaining muscle. Since muscle weighs more than fat, the scales don't accurately reflect what is happening inside you.

Here are some other benefits of combining exercise with healthy eating:

- **Improved cardiovascular health.** Exercise combined with healthy eating decreases your risk of heart disease, which is the number one killer in this country, by lowering blood pressure and cholesterol.

- **Lower stress levels.** Exercise and nutritious foods help you to put the stresses of life into perspective and make for a calmer demeanor, which has been linked with better health.

- **Stronger immune system.** When you exercise regularly and moderately while eating more healthfully, your body is better able to ward off disease.

- **More energy.** A fit body stores more energy, meaning that you have more options in your daily life.

- **Stronger bones.** Exercise and a sound diet help you prevent osteoporosis and the risk of broken bones, both of which typically come with aging.

When you next step on the scales or measure your waist, realize that these numbers aren't telling you the whole story. There are lots of good things happening inside that aren't always reflected in the mirror.

GETTING OLDER MORE SLOWLY

In my work as a coach I spend my days talking with some very fit people. And just like the doctor who sees everyone as being sick, I meet strangers wondering how fit they are. Too often it's easy to see at a glance. Why are so many of us in bad shape? The reasons are obvious: poor diet, eating too much, smoking, excessive alcohol consumption, and lack of exercise.

Nearly all of us were born to be fit and healthy. Most of the degeneration we accept as normal with aging actually results from lack of use. We let our bodies rust out instead of wearing them out. Weak muscles, getting fatter every year, low capacity for physical work, and even life-threatening health issues such as heart disease, some cancers, and high blood pressure can be avoided simply by being active. The problem is that we expect these changes to occur as we get older. When they occur, we see them as inevitable. They aren't.

Low fitness, poor health, obesity, and disease are not normal. Studies of our Stone Age ancestors, who lived more than 10,000 years ago, before the advent of civilization, reveal that they didn't suffer from such maladies even though they did not have a food pyramid, health clubs, personal trainers, or coaches. They ate what was readily available and used their bodies vigorously to cope with the demands of daily life. Even just a few decades ago our health concerns were far different than they are today.

This isn't to say you'll live forever by exercising regularly. A comedian once quipped that his otherwise healthy and ever-exercising grandfather was in the hospital "dying of nothing." But that's not the point. The issue here isn't quantity of life, but rather quality. Life is more enjoyable when you have the capacity to enjoy a wide variety of activities and are free of disease even into what we consider to be old age.

Age also isn't the issue. A study of 80- and 90-year-olds showed that strength and fitness gains can be made at any age given an appropriate program. Hundreds of senior citizens complete marathons, triathlons, and other athletic feats that most younger people consider impossible for themselves. What is holding most people back is motivation, not age. You can't turn back time to reverse your chronological age, but biological age is fully within your control. The key to slowing the aging process is regular exercise.

Chapter 3

YOUR NUTRITION

Many factors determine how well prepared you are for your first triathlon. The three most important are your workouts, sleep, and nutrition. We looked at sleep in Chapter 2. Chapters 5 through 9 and Appendixes B through F cover your workouts and training plan—what to do for exercise and when to do it. That leaves nutrition.

What you eat and when you eat it play big roles in fitness. Food is fuel for your body. The experienced triathlete knows that high-quality foods, eaten in the proper amounts at the right times, make workouts better, speed recovery from workouts, and ultimately contribute to better fitness. This doesn't mean they never splurge and have pizza, a sugary soft drink, or even a doughnut. Each of us has a weakness for certain less-than-healthy foods. For me it's warm brownies, especially fresh from the oven. It's not a matter of *if* I will eat them, but *when.*

This matter of *when* to eat certain types of food is very important for triathlete nutrition. From the perspective of triathlon, the most important event in your day is exercise—your daily workout. Decisions about what to eat must be made based on this daily event more than any other. With this in mind, there are four times, or *phases*, in your day related to what you eat: right before exercise, during exercise, immediately after exercise, and the rest of the day. In this chapter we examine what is best to eat during each of the four phases. (For greater detail on this subject, see my book with Loren Cardain *The Paleo Diet for Athletes.*)

FUELING BEFORE EXERCISE

Doing a workout first thing in the morning may be the best time of day for you, as this is when there are few interruptions. Scientific studies have also shown that people who exercise in the morning are more regular and consistent than those who exercise at any other time of the day. So morning workouts are great for getting in shape.

But the morning isn't always a bed of roses. For one thing, you may be kind of groggy first thing out of bed and find it hard to get going. You may have to force yourself to move along more quickly in the morning, going faster than your legs are prepared to go. In addition, some coaches and athletes believe that your risk of running injuries may be higher in the morning. The warm-up takes longer, so the stress on your joints, muscles, and tendons could be greater.

In a perfect world you'd have something to eat about two hours before starting exercise. This would provide fuel for the workout but would also allow enough time for digestion.

Another problem with morning workouts is eating. In a perfect world you'd have something to eat about two hours before starting exercise. This would provide fuel for the workout but would also allow enough time for digestion. During the night, some of your body's stores of carbohydrate were used up providing fuel for breathing, pumping your heart, moving around in the bed, and other physiological demands of staying alive. If that fuel isn't at least partially replaced, you may feel even more sluggish and low on energy. But you certainly aren't going to get out of bed two hours early just because of this.

If you get up, eat some form of carbohydrates such as cereal, a bagel, or toast, read the paper for a few minutes while sipping a cup of coffee, and then head out the door to swim, bike, or run, digestion won't be given a chance to do its thing. You may start your workout feeling bloated, uncomfortable, and even a bit light-headed.

▶ SPORTS DRINKS, BARS, AND GELS

In the last three decades there has been a profound revolution in sports nutrition. It all started in the 1970s with a sports drink developed at the University of Florida—Gatorade. There are now more products on the market than can be sampled in a four-hour workout. The field has expanded well beyond drinks consumed during exercise. Now there are carbohydrate-loading drinks, recovery drinks, sports bars, and energy gels. These include various combinations of sugars, protein, fat, electrolytes, caffeine, vitamins, minerals, and other scientific-sounding ingredients. It's getting confusing. To help clear the haze, here's a short primer.

Sports Drinks

Researchers at the University of Florida launched this product category in 1965 when they created a drink, which they later named Gatorade, for the school's football team. Before Gatorade, athletes were discouraged from drinking any fluids at all during exercise, including water. Today this is unthinkable. Sports drinks today always include a sugar and usually also have some amount of sodium. Besides the fluid, these are the most critical components of any sports drink. There are all sorts of other ingredients as well, including other minerals (e.g., potassium, magnesium, and calcium), caffeine, protein, fat, amino acids, and vitamins. Sports drinks are critical for long and highly intense workouts and races.

Sports Bars

In the mid-1980s PowerBar launched a new category of sports nutritionals—sports bars. Although they look much like a candy bar, the primary ingredient is usually carbohydrates, and all contain some fat and protein. Most have fewer than three grams of fat, although some have twice that amount. Others are relatively high in protein

continued ➔

Sports Drinks, Bars, and Gels *(continued)*

or carbohydrates. Most sports bar companies make more than one type of bar, so read the package carefully to make sure you are getting what you want. Examples are PowerBar, Clif Bar, and Balance Bar.

Bars should be used in low-intensity exercise lasting longer than about ninety minutes—three to four hours or longer is probably appropriate. The major limiter for these products is their absorption rate. You must drink 8 to 16 ounces of fluid with every bar eaten, and it still may take thirty minutes or more for the fuel to get to your working muscles.

Gels

The newest entry, first appearing in the mid-1990s, is energy gels—gooey liquids that come in ketchup-sized pouches to be torn open and sucked out. Their main attraction is the convenience of a small package and a high energy yield—about 100 calories per packet. In this category are PowerGel, Accel Gel, Carb-BOOM, Gu, Hammer Gel, Lava Gel, and Clif Shot. During exercise lasting an hour or more, take one gel packet every thirty minutes. Be sure to drink 8 to 10 ounces of water with each packet. During events lasting four hours or longer, consume a packet every fifteen minutes, especially later in the event.

Be careful to take in enough water when using sports bars and gels. If you don't, your gut will pull fluid from your blood to help in the digestive process. This can result in dehydration. ⊗

The light-headed feeling results from how the body reacts to starchy foods. It pumps insulin into the bloodstream to move the sugar from the foods you just ate into your muscles and liver to restock the stores depleted during the night. But when insulin is faced with a flood of sugar from starchy foods, it tends to overreact and aggressively removes nearly all sugar from the blood, leaving you hypoglycemic—low on blood sugar. And since your brain uses sugar as its primary fuel source, when there isn't much available, you feel light-headed.

One way to resolve this problem is to take in nothing but water or unsweetened coffee or tea until ten minutes before you start exercising. As you're putting on your swim goggles, pumping up your tires, or lacing up your running shoes, sip a sports drink or take some gel with water. But be sure to start your workout no more than ten minutes after you consume the sports drink or gel. Ten minutes is not enough time for the body to send insulin out to do its job, so you start the workout with a few more calories in your body and no drop in blood sugar. Once exercise begins the body deals with sugar in a different way, so insulin no longer presents a problem.

If you are not one to exercise first thing in the morning, you can eat something a couple of hours before the workout with little possibility of a downside. This could be a light meal with an emphasis on carbohydrates, especially from fruits and vegetables. If your stomach tends to be a bit squeamish during exercise even with a couple of hours separating your meal and your swim, bike, or run, you may need to eat pre-workout foods that are soft, low in fiber, and easily digested, such as unsweetened applesauce, a banana, sports food supplements (such as GatorPro), liquid meals in a bottle (such as Ensure), and a sports bar with water. I've even known triathletes to use baby food, which is easy to digest.

In Chapter 11 we'll take a look at eating on the morning of your race. At that time your stomach is likely to be a bit uneasy, so these easily digested foods will be good options. Experimenting with them before workouts will help you find out what will work best at the race.

The key to pre-workout eating is finding foods that work for you. There are many options when it comes to the combination of food and exercise. Once you find what works for you, stick with it. Warning signs that you haven't found the right foods or that you're eating too close to your workouts are an upset stomach, diarrhea, light-headedness, low energy, or early fatigue during exercise. Be aware that a cause of these symptoms may also be that you simply ate too much, even if it was two hours prior to exercise. About 400 calories, give or take a few depending on your size and tolerance for food first thing in the morning, is about right. If you eat less than two hours before exercise, reduce the calories. A rule of thumb is to eat about 200 calories for each hour before you begin working out. See Table 3.1 for sample pre-workout foods that may work for you before workouts and races, along with their caloric content.

TABLE 3.1	WHAT TO EAT BEFORE A WORKOUT

Real Food	Calories
Applesauce, unsweetened (1 cup)	194
Banana (medium size)	105
Oatmeal (1 packet)	104
Potato, baked	220
Fruit smoothie	200–400

Meal Supplement Drinks	Calories
EAS Myoplex Plus (16 oz.)	280
Endura Optimizer (12 oz.)	280
Endurox R4 (12 oz.)	280
Ensure (8 oz.)	250
GatorPro (11 oz.)	370
Metabolol II (12 oz.)	260
Met-Rx Original (16 oz.)	60
OptiFuel 2 (12 oz.)	480

Meal Supplement Bars	Calories
Balance Bar	190
Clif Builder's Bar	270
Met-Rx Protein Plus	330
PowerBar Pria	110

FUELING DURING EXERCISE

During exercise the body has two primary sources of fuel—its onboard stores of fat and carbohydrates. Each of us has plenty of fat and would gladly use it for fuel. But the body likes to save its fat, only increasing its reliance on that "tank" as the duration of your exercise increases. The less fit you are, the more it avoids burning fat. As you get in better aerobic shape, more fat is used for fuel during exercise. As the old saying goes, "The rich get richer and the poor get poorer!"

So when you first start a triathlon training program, your body will use a lot of carbohydrates to fuel exercise. Before getting into what this fuel source is all about, let me answer that nagging question, "If I'm not using much fat during exercise and I'm not in very good shape now, how will I ever lose weight by exercising?" The answer is in the sidebar "The Fat-Burning Zone Myth." A one-sentence summary: More calories are burned after exercise as your metabolism speeds up

---

▶ THE FAT-BURNING ZONE MYTH

For years we have been told that there is a low-intensity, fat-burning zone, and that if we exercise at that level of intensity we'll lose weight faster than at any other level of intensity. This myth is so well established that it may never go away. But I'll keep trying to dispel it anyway.

It really doesn't matter how much fat you burn during exercise, but how much is burned during recovery following exercise. Extensive research backs this up. For example, one study examined the relative benefits of low- and high-intensity exercise for fat loss (Tremblay et al., 1994). In the low-intensity group of subjects, eight men and nine women pedaled four or five times each week for twenty weeks. Their intensity, based on heart rate, could be described as easy to moderate—the "fat-burning zone." The high-intensity group, made up of five men and five women, pedaled the same number of days each week, but for only fifteen weeks. Their sessions lasted

continued ➔

The Fat-Burning Zone Myth *(continued)*

just long enough to include a warm-up, intervals, and a cool-down. The intervals were fifteen to ninety seconds long and done at a very high level of effort, with long recoveries between the intervals.

The low-intensity group used more than twice as many calories during each of their exercise sessions as the high-intensity group. Yet when it came time to check body fatness with calipers, the high-intensity pedalers had lost significantly more fat. The reason for this is that following the more intense exercise sessions, their metabolism stayed high for much longer than that of the moderate pedalers. Other research has shown that one intense workout can increase a person's resting metabolic rate for up to thirty-six hours. So more total fat is burned after high-intensity exercise, with most of it melting off during rest. The scientists confirmed what was happening by measuring the enzymes that burn fat. They were greatly elevated in the high-intensity subjects, but there was no change in the low-intensity folks.

The bottom line for all of this is that you should forget about the "fat-burning zone" during exercise. Such thinking is counterproductive. Going slow for a long time won't make you svelte.

than during exercise, and these post-workout calories come primarily from fat due to an increase in your resting metabolic rate (discussed in Chapter 2).

Although even the fittest triathlete has a lot of calories stored as fat in his or her body, enough calories to fuel even an Ironman-distance triathlon and then some, none of us has a lot of carbohydrates packed away. Let's take a skinny male triathlete who weighs 150 pounds and has 7 percent body fat. That's a little more than 10 pounds of fat. Each pound of fat is about 3,500 calories, so our lean friend theoretically has more than 35,000 calories available just from his fat. If it were possible for him to use fat only during his Ironman race, and he burned 700 calories per hour for the 10 hours it takes him to finish, he could do the race five times nonstop without running out of energy—and without refueling.

This will never happen because of the other fuel—carbohydrates. We don't have very much onboard. Carbohydrates are stored in the liver and all of the muscles throughout the body as "glycogen." Carbohydrates in the blood are called "glucose." You have perhaps 1,500 to 2,000 calories in this tank, depending on your size and fitness level. Big people and aerobically fit athletes store more of this precious commodity.

While 1,500 to 2,000 calories may sound like a lot, it really isn't. If our skinny triathlete used only carbohydrates to fuel his exercise, he would last for a little more than two hours. That's hardly enough to finish an Ironman. To make matters worse for him, all of the carbohydrates are not available, since not every muscle is used when, for example, he is riding his bike. The glycogen in his arms, upper back, face, and other body parts is not being called on to provide fuel for the body even though a lot is needed by the legs. The carbohydrates stored in the arms simply refuse to make the pilgrimage to the legs to provide fuel. So our friend is forced to rely on the carbohydrates stored just in his leg muscles, unless he takes in some carbohydrates during the race. More on this later.

In the real world the body never relies on just one of these fuel sources; it is always using some mix of both. When you are going slow and easy, fat is the primary fuel, but some amount of carbohydrates is still contributing calories. (Again, be sure to read "The Fat-Burning Zone Myth" sidebar.) As you start exercising faster and harder, the body shifts to more reliance on carbohydrates, although some fat is still being used.

The body simply cannot operate on one fuel only. If you start to run low on one of them—carbohydrates, obviously—it simply will not go on. This is referred to as "bonking." The way to prevent the bonk is to take in carbohydrates both before and during exercise. We've already looked at fueling before exercise, so now let's examine what to take in while you're working out.

If before your workout you consumed some food, sports drink, or gel with water, and your workout will last less than an hour, as most will in the training plan in Chapter 9, all you need to take in during the exercise session is water. It's okay to use a sports drink in this situation, but it is not necessary. For longer workouts or for those that start early in the morning after an overnight fast, it's a good idea to use a product designed for use during exercise. Don't use fruit juice, as the fructose in it moves to the muscles very slowly. It could also upset your stomach during exercise. Also, don't use plain water if your workout will take more than an hour.

You only need 16 to 24 ounces of sports drink per hour while exercising, depending on your size, how hard you are working, and the weather. On hot or humid days you will need more than on cooler days. I recommend using a sports drink instead of gels with water. It's too easy to get the gel-water mix wrong. Too much gel with too little water creates the risk of dehydrating as your body pulls fluids into the stomach and intestines to digest the carbohydrates. Just be sure to mix the sports drink to the concentration recommended on the label.

For the same reason, you won't need to use sports bars or energy bars during exercise. These bars are slow to get carbohydrates to the working muscles and need a lot of water to wash them down. I don't recommend bars for the athletes I coach until their workouts or races are four or more hours long. Here's a summary of how to refuel during exercise:

Exercise duration	Water	Sports drink	Gels	Energy bars
Under one hour with pre-workout fuel	x			
Under one hour with no pre-workout fuel	x	x		
1–4 hours	x	x		
4 or more hours	x	x	x	x

REFUELING AFTER EXERCISE

Immediately after exercise your body has two primary needs—water and carbohydrates. To a lesser extent it also needs essential amino acids and electrolytes, especially sodium. For workouts that are long, highly intense, or hot, you'll need more of each of these. The sooner you consume them after stopping, the sooner you will be ready for the next workout. I tell the athletes I coach that refueling is their highest priority right after exercise. Within the first thirty minutes, before stretching, taking a shower, or anything else, they start refueling. At this time the body is better primed to accept and restock carbohydrates in the muscles and liver than at any other time in the day.

Following a long or difficult workout or race, use something a bit more potent than a sports drink, gel, or bar. You can purchase commercial recovery drinks, but they can be made quite a bit cheaper in your own kitchen. See my recipe below for a fruit smoothie that can be used after workouts lasting less than one hour.

RECOVERY DRINK

8–12 oz. fruit juice of your choice

1 serving fruit (such as a banana or frozen berries)

1–2 pinches table salt

1–2 teaspoons protein powder

1–2 handfuls ice

Puree in a blender. This makes a drink of about 250 to 300 calories. For longer and harder workouts, you can add 1 tablespoon of table sugar, which is about 50 calories.

When shopping for protein powder, look first for egg protein. This may be hard to find, so the next best option is egg and whey protein or whey alone. Third best is soy powder. It's best not to use vegetable protein powder, as it is missing several essential amino acids needed for recovery.

An hour or so after a one-hour workout and drinking a recovery drink, it's time to move on to regular food. If you're an experienced swimmer, biker, or runner, and you complete a much longer and harder workout, you may well need another recovery drink and more time to recover before sitting down to a meal. In this case, figure that for every minute of exercise you will spend one minute in this short-term recovery phase taking in a recovery drink and starchy foods such as a potato, cereal, bread, a bagel, rice, pasta, or corn. These foods are rich in glucose, a form of sugar that the body uses to quickly replace its workout-depleted stores of carbohydrates.

But if you're not doing difficult workouts longer than an hour, use only the recovery drink in the first thirty minutes after stopping and then, later on, have a meal of real food. Don't rely on recovery foods, sports bars, gels, or energy drinks beyond this point in your day. Not only will they add unwanted body weight, they are also low in the micronutrients—vitamins and minerals—necessary for good health and fitness.

EATING DURING THE REST OF THE DAY

Up to this point the emphasis of before, during, and after exercise nutrition has been on carbohydrates, especially from sugar-rich sources such as sports drinks, gels, and bars, and also starchy foods. The purpose of all this sugar is to keep your muscle and liver glycogen stores up so that you don't run out. If you've done a good job, you don't need to be as concerned with quick-acting forms of carbohydrates during the rest of the day.

After your initial recovery from exercise, the emphasis shifts to eating foods that are rich in all of the essential nutrients. This includes essential amino acids from protein-rich foods, carbohydrates with lots of vitamins and minerals, and healthy fats.

Essential Amino Acids

Amino acids make up protein, which is found in almost all foods but especially in animal products such as fish, poultry, red meat, and eggs. My experience in working with athletes for more than two decades is that they tend to eat too little protein because they focus their diets on sugar and starch. That's too bad, because the amino acids in protein are necessary for the growth, repair, and maintenance of your muscles and other cells. I've come to realize that athletes who eat too little protein will recover slowly after workouts, are easily injured, and never achieve their full potential in triathlons. You can't skimp on protein if you want to get in shape.

Scientists have identified twenty amino acids necessary for human development. Eight of these are essential amino acids because your adult body can't make them. Animal foods are rich in these essentials, while plant foods are each lacking in some of them. But it's possible to combine plant foods to prepare a meal that has all of the essential amino acids. A common way some vegetarians do this is to mix beans and grains together (for example, beans and rice or peanut butter and bread). The downside is that you have to eat a lot more vegetable food to get the same amount of essential amino acids that are in animal foods. For example, one roasted turkey breast has 14,290 milligrams of essential amino acids in a 4-ounce serving. To get the same amount from a meal of black beans and rice, you'd have to eat two cups of rice and two cups of beans. That's a lot of beans and rice. And there are nearly five times as many calories in the beans and rice (864) as in the turkey (179).

Unless you need to gain a lot of weight (and really like beans!), the surest way to provide your body with the building supplies needed to get into shape is to eat animal products. This doesn't mean you should cut out vegetables, however, as they are rich in vitamins and minerals.

Vitamins and Minerals

When most people talk about carbohydrates they mean starchy foods such as cereal, bread, bagels, rice, corn, and potatoes. While these are indeed carbohydrate-based foods, they make up only one part of this food category. We tend to forget that fruits and vegetables are also in the carbohydrate group. We need more of these foods, especially vegetables, in our meals after the thirty-minute recovery period following the day's last workout, because veggies have more vitamins and minerals than any other foods you could eat.

Because vitamins and minerals are necessary to promote growth and to maintain health, if your diet is deficient in them you run the risk of a slow response to training and perhaps even disease. People who eat a lot of food every day and never exercise don't have to worry about this, but if you are watching your calories and exercising a lot, the risk is greater.

Vegetables in general have far more vitamins and minerals than any other food group. Spinach has 65 percent more calcium per calorie than milk does; broccoli, rhubarb, turnip greens, and watercress also have more calcium per calorie than milk. Other minerals necessary for strenuous exercise, such as iron, magnesium, phosphorous, potassium, and zinc, are also found in great quantities in vegetables. In addition, veggies are loaded with the exercise-critical B vitamins and antioxidants such as vitamins E and C. As a group, vegetables have several times as much vitamins and minerals as any other food group.

On the whole, the food groups with the least vitamins and minerals are whole grains, dairy, seeds, and nuts. This doesn't mean to never eat these foods. But if you are exercising strenuously and watching your calories, you want to eat mostly micronutrient-dense foods.

Healthy Fats

We've been taught that fat is bad for our health and told to restrict it in our diets. It isn't the amount of fat in your diet that is the problem, but rather the type of fat. Fat is necessary for immune system health and adds a pleasing flavor and texture to food. You just need to be aware of and control how much you eat when it comes to the three "bad" fats—saturated, trans fat, and polyunsaturated omega-6 oil. These fats have been shown to contribute to health problems such as heart disease, skin cancer, diabetes, and asthma. They just aren't good for anyone, whether a triathlete or a couch spud.

ⓘ ENERGIZING EXERCISE

Where does the energy for exercise come from? Knowing the answer to this question will help you make decisions about how to exercise to achieve certain benefits, and how to recover from workouts. The majority of the fuel the body uses to create energy comes from three sources—fat, carbohydrates, and creatine phosphate. Let's examine the role each plays in exercise.

Fat is the major fuel for all endurance exercise. "Endurance" means continuous exercise lasting longer than about two minutes. Even the skinniest athlete has several hours of energy stored in his or her body as fat.

Carbohydrates are stored as either "glycogen" in the muscles and liver or "glucose" in the blood. Glycogen makes up most of this energy source, but it is quite limited. A well-conditioned athlete may have enough for 2 to 3 hours of intense exercise socked away. When glycogen begins to run low, exercise must slow down, regardless of how much fat is still available. This is one reason why it is so important to take in carbohydrate-based sports drinks during workouts lasting longer than about an hour.

Creatine phosphate is a quick-burning fuel stored in the muscles that lasts only a few seconds—perhaps 8 to 12. A sudden increase in effort, such as a sprint at the end of a race or a short, powerful hill climb, relies on this fuel.

This discussion may make it sound as if the body throws switches to change from one energy source to another. That's not the case. There is considerable overlap between the fuels used in a single workout, with the percentages fluctuating in relation to intensity, warm-up, and fitness level.

As endurance exercise begins, the first few seconds are fueled primarily by creatine phosphate as the fat and glycogen processing mechanisms kick in. In the next few minutes—perhaps 10 to 30—glycogen supplies much of the energy, with

continued ➔

Energizing Exercise *(continued)*

---

fat slowly increasing its contribution, if the workout is a steady effort. Eventually, fat becomes the predominant fuel source for long and slow exercise, with glycogen adding most of the balance.

This doesn't mean that slow exercise is the best way to burn fat; the total energy expenditure during light activity is low when compared with fast and intense workouts. Although the percentage of fat burned in intense exercise—such as intervals—is smaller, the total energy used is larger, potentially producing a great amount of total fat use.

These bad fats are found in such food sources as feedlot-raised and factory-farmed animals, snack foods, packaged meals, margarine, and dairy, and in such ubiquitous products as peanut butter, bread, bagels, salad dressing, and frozen vegetables. When you shop, read the labels carefully and avoid those products listing saturated fat and partially hydrogenated fat and those made with vegetable oils such as soybean, peanut, cottonseed, safflower, sunflower, sesame, and corn. You'll find this cuts out a lot of foods. But you'll quickly become familiar with the best packaged foods.

The fats you should get more of in your diet are monounsaturated fat and polyunsaturated omega-3 oil as these meet your daily need for fat and promote good health. These are found in nuts, especially macadamias and walnuts, avocados, olive oil, canola oil, cold-water fish (such as salmon, mackerel, herring, halibut, cod, and tuna), leafy green vegetables, and flaxseed oil. Not only will you be healthier for eating these fats, but you'll also improve your aerobic fitness, recover from exercise faster, and possibly reduce post-exercise soreness. I advise the athletes I coach to supplement their diets with fish oil capsules, because it is difficult to completely avoid the bad fats.

Chapter 4

YOUR SUPPORT

This book relies heavily on the word *your*, as in *your diet, your lifestyle*, and *your training plan*. I hope this doesn't lead you to believe that you should do it alone by becoming an athletic hermit living in a cave, coming out only to swim, bike, and run. Although triathlon is ultimately an individual sport requiring self-sufficiency, it doesn't have to be a lonely sport. You'll find that triathletes, as a whole, are fun, gregarious people who love to be with others. And if you want to succeed in the sport, you will certainly need the help of others—your supporters.

EMOTIONAL SUPPORT

On the whole, training for a triathlon is a great pleasure. Realizing that your fitness is improving, your waistline is trimming, and you can handle more exercise is highly motivating. But there will be times when none of this seems to be happening and you are also weary and have too many responsibilities to manage. At these times you need the emotional support of family and friends to keep going. Without their support and encouragement, you're likely to fall off the wagon.

Family

Your spouse is your most important supporter. I once coached a runner who wanted to qualify for the Boston Marathon and had a chance, although he was going to have to run his best race ever to do it. His wife, however, thought that running was just plain dumb. She gave him a hard time whenever he went out to run. So he got in the habit of getting out of bed several hours early on Saturdays so he could get his long run done and be back by the time his wife woke up. Whenever possible he hid his running from her. He had no support at home for his goal. Needless to say, he did not qualify despite his hard work.

The most supportive spouses are often those who also are physically active. They can empathize with their triathletic husbands and wives. But I also know many spouses who are 100 percent supportive even though they never swim, bike, or run. You can foster such support by sharing in your spouse's dreams and aspirations. Being honestly enthusiastic about your other half's activities is the starting point. Be sure to make him or her a part of your team by sharing your experiences and achievements and asking for help whenever you need it. You can also wrap a family vacation around a triathlon so the whole family gets involved.

Friends

There's no getting around it—triathletes are unusual people. We carefully avoid unhealthy food, exercise before and after work, enjoy sweating, talk incessantly about our last workout, and ogle fast bikes the way a starving man looks at food. Only other triathletes can fully understand such strange behavior. Yet there are nontriathletes who continue to hang out with us happily and even feign an interest in our obsession. We call these people *friends*. You need lots of them if you're to make it in triathlon. They may not always understand what we are talking about, but they always care and are there when we need them. Such people are truly good friends whose support we must carefully nurture. So don't lay it all on them at once—and realize that they may have something of interest in their lives also. Support works both ways. You must be willing to go the extra mile for a friend who supports you. This may occasionally mean making the ultimate sacrifice—missing a workout. You get back in direct proportion to how much you give.

MOTIVATIONAL SUPPORT

Triathlon can be a lonely sport. It's really nice to occasionally have someone along for a workout. A steady diet of solo exercise can be mind-numbing, or worse—it can contribute to a loss of motivation. It's a rare person who can do every workout alone and stay enthusiastic. A training partner, or better yet, a group, is the best therapy for boredom and low motivation.

Clubs

Many larger cities and even some small ones have triathlon clubs. These groups often offer weekly workouts in one or more of the three disciplines. They usually have newsletters containing information of local interest. Their periodic meetings might feature speakers. Some even have club coaches who can help you grow as a triathlete. You can find out whether there's a triathlon club in your area by going to the USA Triathlon Federation Web site, www.usatriathlon.org, clicking first on "Clubs," and then "Find a Club." Or ask other triathletes you know and the staff at local sporting goods stores. If there isn't a club in your area, consider starting one. For assistance, contact the USA Triathlon Federation through its Web site.

Training Partners

If there just aren't any clubs in your area, finding another triathlete of your ability will do wonders for your motivation. You will discover that it's easier to get out of bed in the morning or go for an after-work training session if you know your training partner will be there, too. In the winter months, getting together with a training partner for an indoor bike-trainer ride or side-by-side treadmill run will boost not only the quality but also the enjoyment of such workouts.

Again, a local store frequented by triathletes may be just the ticket to finding someone. Some shops provide a bulletin board where you can post a looking-for-a-training-partner note.

TECHNICAL SUPPORT

Getting in shape, dealing with or preventing injuries, and buying and maintaining the right equipment are all huge tasks. Each is so complex that it is impossible for an individual to keep up with even the most basic technical information. Specialists are the answer.

Shops

Once upon a time, sporting goods stores that specialized in swim, bike, or run gear were the unchallenged center of the triathlon universe. That's where you went to buy anything needed for the sport. That is no longer the case. Mail-order and online catalogs have made it difficult for many of these specialty stores to stay in business. Those that have succeeded have made it by offering a lot more than just equipment; they also offer information, quality bicycle repair and maintenance, and other specialized services. Good shops will also make sure you buy the right stuff in a world of ever increasing equipment complexity. This is also the place to go for event flyers, to get training questions answered, or to have your bike adjusted to help an aching knee.

If you enjoy receiving these services, it behooves you to make your purchases at such a local shop. The prices are not significantly higher than catalog or online costs with shipping added on. Even if you spend a couple of dollars more, the services you get are certainly worth the small extra expense.

Medical Examinations

When I start coaching an athlete, one of the first things I do is have him or her see a physical therapist for a thorough orthopedic exam. I want to know where the weak links are and what we can do to prevent injury. The most common problems found, even in otherwise seemingly sound athletes, are poor spinal health, unstable knees, muscle imbalances, leg-length discrepancies, flat feet, and poor posture. The therapist can suggest strength and flexibility exercises to alleviate the negative consequences of such conditions. I find this to be an invaluable step in preventing injuries and optimizing performance. It's money very well spent when you're just starting out.

It helps if your doctor also exercises or at least understands why you do and supports it. It used to be that when a patient came in complaining of a sore knee from running, the doctor would prescribe aspirin and suggest no more such foolishness as jogging. Now sports medicine is a booming business, and if your doctor doesn't know exactly how to handle your aches and pains, he or she can refer you to a sports specialist. The world of triathlon is much better because of this development in medicine.

Coach

The field of triathlon coaching is growing larger every year. What was once a hobby for a few has become a career for many. The USA Triathlon Federation, the governing body of the sport in the United States, now lists nearly a thousand certified triathlon coaches on its Web site (www.usatriathlon.org). At this site you can find a coach to help you grow as a triathlete. I recommend finding someone who lives in your area, since you are new to the sport and will need face-to-face coaching as you develop skills. Once you are skilled and have more experience, there are many more coaches available who work via the Internet. You can find coaches I have trained at www.ultrafit.com.

Coaching fees vary considerably, from free to hundreds of dollars a month. You typically get just what you pay for, so don't let price be the only determining factor. It's a good idea to interview at least three before making a final selection. You'll find there are considerable differences in the services they offer. You will also probably find that you relate best to one of them. That's the one for you.

Besides designing and refining a training plan for you, a good coach will provide advice on equipment purchases, diet, race strategy, and motivation. In fact, just having a coach is usually good for motivation. He or she is part of your team.

INFORMATIONAL SUPPORT

Triathlon is one of the youngest sports in the world, having been around only since the 1970s. In the 1980s and 1990s the number of participants and races grew steadily, but following its Olympic debut in the 2000 Sydney Games, growth has been exponential. In the United States there were 53,000 USA Triathlon Federation–licensed triathletes in 2004 and perhaps that many again who participate in local triathlons without getting an annual license.

Due to its recent rapid growth, information on the sport is overwhelming. It's impossible to keep up with all of it, so pick a couple of sources from the following suggestions and use them to learn more about your sport.

Cyberspace

A Google search on "triathlon" will yield millions of results. Newsgroups, bulletin boards, blogs, Web sites, chat rooms, online magazines, and live talks by experts abound. It isn't possible to list all of them here, but following are a few that may prove helpful:

- **Race calendars.** Are you planning a vacation and want to see if there's a triathlon you could do at your destination? Or perhaps you just want to see what's available in your region. Three good Internet sites for this information are www.active.com/triathlon/, http://alpha.fordhamllc.com/calendar/, and www.cooltri.com/calendar1.htm. Here you can both find a race listing and complete an entry form online.

- **General triathlon information.** Want to see what others also new to the sport are doing as they prepare for a triathlon? Go to www.trinewbies.com. For basic information on training, race reports, and firsthand experiences, go to www.hulaman.com. This is the oldest free triathlon training site on the Web. The single largest discussion site for triathletes on all matters related to the sport is at http://groups.google.com/group/rec.sport.triathlon.

- **Coaching.** For assistance finding a triathlon coach, go to www.yourfirst tri.com. For a list of all USA Triathlon–certified coaches, point your Web browser at www.usatriathlon.org/coaches/coaches_find_frames.htm.
- **Training log.** One of the best sites for storing and analyzing your training data, and also a place where you can get your triathlon questions answered by a real coach, is www.trainingpeaks.com.

Print Media

Although triathlon sites on the World Wide Web are prodigious, print media on this topic in the United States are rather limited. Two magazines dominate the national scene: *Inside Triathlon* and *Triathlete*. *Inside Triathlon*, the newer of the two, focuses its coverage on triathletes by age group. *Triathlete* has been around since the early 1980s and provides extensive coverage of professional racing plus age-group coverage. Both are available on magazine racks or can be subscribed to online (www.insidetri.com and www.triathletemag.com). In addition, many regional publications focus on triathlon, such as *Colorado Triathlete, SoCal Tri-Life, Rocky Mountain Sports, Windy City Sports, Competitor,* and *Oklahoma Runner & Triathlete*. These are usually available in sporting goods stores and health clubs and on newsstands.

Chapter 5

YOUR SWIMMING

Of the three triathlon sports, you'll spend the least amount of time swimming, both during training and in the race. This is partly because the swim is so short in a sprint triathlon—usually around 400 meters. The biking and running legs will last a lot longer in the race. The swim is kind of like a warm-up for the rest of the triathlon. Your goal for the swim leg of the race is just to finish it; it doesn't matter what your time is. You may stop several times to catch your breath. That's okay; others will stop, too.

Swim training is mostly about learning good technique, whereas training for the bike and run is mostly about building fitness. What we want to accomplish with your swimming at this stage of your triathlon career is not developing speed or great endurance, but rather developing sound swimming skills—something to build on for the future.

If you are already a swimmer, this will be a breeze. You've got a great start on becoming a triathlete, because it takes months, if not years, to hone the mechanics of swimming. Just be careful not to spend most of your training time in the pool. Triathletes tend to gravitate toward what comes easiest while avoiding their weaker sports. As an accomplished swimmer, you should spend more time on the bike and run than those without a swim background.

FORM—NOT FITNESS

Getting started in swimming is mostly about learning to swim properly. You can probably already swim now, meaning that you can take a few strokes without sinking and may even be able to complete one length of the pool. But most people at this stage have poor technique because they developed bad habits when they first learned to swim.

As a kid your only goal in going to the pool was to have fun with others in the water. You didn't care how much energy it took to swim after a ball or chase your buddies. But these swimming flaws will come back to haunt you while training for your first triathlon. Poor technique uses up a lot more energy than is necessary, causing you to start the bike section of the race already feeling drained.

Flaws

Face out of Water

It's normal for mammals to keep their heads and faces out of the water when swimming, for example as a dog does. Since we don't have gills and the air is above the water, that makes sense. This will be your biggest challenge in learning to swim and is the starting place for learning good technique. Throughout your triathlon career you'll hear athletes and swim instructors talking about how to breathe, when to breathe, and how often to breathe.

Throughout your triathlon career you'll hear athletes and swim instructors talking about how to breathe, when to breathe, and how often to breathe.

Hips below Shoulders

Because your face is out of the water, a line drawn from your shoulders through your hips would be slanted down, with your hips low in the water. In this position it takes more energy to move forward because you are presenting a lot of frontal area to the water. Water is a thick, resistant medium that causes you to work harder. Once you learn to put your face in the water and breathe correctly, your hips will come up, and you'll be amazed at how much easier it is to swim. It's like the difference between pushing a sheet of plywood through the water horizontally and doing it vertically.

Pushing Down on the Water

In order to keep their faces above the water line, novices push down on the water with their hands. This results in very little forward movement. Again, learning to swim and breathe with your face in the water will go a long way toward correcting this common fault.

Kicking Too Much

Since their hands and arms aren't providing much forward movement, novices kick hard to go forward. In this position the kick is not very effective, so it requires more effort. Once you learn to swim horizontally, you'll find that the kick is only needed to provide balance—not locomotion. With your body in a streamlined position, your hands and arms will do most of the work to move you forward.

Good Technique

The starting place for developing good swim technique is learning to put your face in the water and breathe to the side. Once you can do this everything else will fall into place. At that point you will be working on refining technique and becoming smoother and more efficient. For now you're tackling the major skill—head position and breathing. The best way to learn this is with an instructor. I do not recommend doing it alone.

The best choice for instruction is to hire a swim instructor and take a lesson once or twice a week. You will develop skills quickly with a good teacher. Do not ask a friend who is a good swimmer; he or she probably will not be a good swim teacher. Look for someone with lots of experience working with newbies.

Some instructors offer swim instruction over the Internet. They ask you to have someone use an underwater camera to make a movie of you swimming and then send it to them; an instructor analyzes it and sends you technique tips. This is much less effective than having a real, live coach watching, but if you don't have any other options, it can point you in the right direction.

Even though you have an instructor, you'll need to practice on your own to really develop your skills. Following the training schedules provided in Chapter 9 will give you that opportunity.

The next best instruction option is to swim with a masters group at your health club, community pool, or YMCA. Ask around to see what's available. This is usually the least expensive route to take. Be careful not to join a highly competitive, advanced group. Look for one that caters to beginners. Swim groups usually have a coach on deck who can provide feedback on your technique; ask the coach to help you whenever possible. But you are not the only person in the pool, so you won't get lots of personal attention.

A third instruction option is to attend a swim camp. Triathlon and swim coaches offer camps regionally. Two of the best known are Terry Laughlin (www. totalimmersion.net) and Steve Tarpinian (www.swimpower.com/2000/cac.cfm). You can read about their camp offerings online to see if there is one in your area. While you're online, also check out the great visual aid "Cyber Swimmer" at www.icanpledge.com/swimmer/default.htm.

Even with an instructor and practice, it's a good idea to learn as much as you can about swim technique. Books and videos available at retailers and online will help you see what good form looks like.

Always remember that your goal for swimming right now is not to become more fit, but rather to learn to swim with good technique. As you work on your swimming skills your fitness will improve without a lot of hard work. In fact, overworking during a swim workout at this stage is likely to cause your form to break down and reinforce your old flaws. Form—not fitness!

WHERE TO SWIM

For beginners I recommend swimming in a public pool, such as at your health club, city facility, or YMCA. Even if you have a pool in your backyard you'll find that you improve faster with others around. In part, this is because you will learn

▶ SWIMMING IN OPEN WATER

If your triathlon will be in a lake or the ocean you need to develop open-water swim skills. A word of caution: Never swim alone in open water. Always have at least one partner who stays close. This is something I require even with the pro triathletes I coach.

The first skill to learn in open-water swimming is sighting on fixed objects so that you swim a straight line. The rougher the water is, the more of a challenge this is. Every fifth stroke or so, raise your head to be sure your progress relative to the landmark is correct. This landmark may be a tall building, tree, pier, or something similar. In the race it may be a large buoy. It's best to have several such objects you can use for navigating during your swim. ⊛

from watching others who have mastered the techniques. Having others around also makes swimming safer.

At this stage in your budding triathlon career, open-water swimming, such as in lakes or the ocean, is best avoided. Not only is open water inherently risky, but such swimming also makes it more difficult to develop good technique. A controlled pool environment with calm water, a black line to follow, and lane ropes to keep you corralled provides just enough structure to keep you focused on form. There are too many variables in open water to allow you to concentrate on stroke mechanics.

Understanding and following pool etiquette is necessary to make swimming safe and enjoyable for everyone. Space is limited in a lap pool. The lanes are narrow and there may be a lot of swimmers trying to use them. Unwritten pool etiquette rules help the pool handle lots of people. Following are the more common rules; if there is any confusion about the specific rules where you are swimming, check with a lifeguard.

- **Rule 1: Choose an appropriate lane.** If the pool is busy, there may be signs at the lanes specifying pace. The signs could be as simple as "Fast," "Medium," and "Slow," or they might be designated by swim pace, such as 1:30 per 100 yards for one lane and 1:45 per 100 yards in the next lane. If there aren't any designations, assess which lane has swimmers in it who are going about your pace. If there are open lanes without reserved signs or something similar, feel free to take any one of them.

- **Rule 2: Enter the water safely.** Don't dive in. Not only is it unsafe, it's also rude. Lower yourself into the water feet first or go down a ladder. If there is someone else in the lane, stand to the side until you are certain you have been seen, before starting. Give the other person plenty of time to establish a gap and then begin swimming.

- **Rule 3: Share the lane.** If you're entering a lane that has one other swimmer in it, ask if he or she wants to split the lane, each keeping to a side, or swim a circle, staying to the right. The first person in the lane "owns" it, so don't assume without asking. If you're the third to enter the lane and there are two already splitting it, stand to the side and wait for an opportunity to ask if you can share their lane and swim a circle. Circle swimming is almost always done counterclockwise by staying as close as possible to the lane rope on the right, with the black line on the bottom of the pool serving as a lane divider.

- **Rule 4: Pass politely.** If someone wants to pass you in the pool when swimming circles, he or she will touch you on the foot. Do not stop—continue swimming. This is just your signal that at the next wall you should stay right, pause in the corner, and let the faster swimmer make the turn to your left. If you are the "passer," touch the other person's foot only once. Repeated touching is annoying.

- **Rule 5: Stay out of the way when resting.** It's okay to stop and take a breather, but stop only at a wall, and squeeze into the right-hand corner of the lane next to the rope. If you're going to pause for several minutes, get out of the pool.

- **Rule 6: Ask before using pool equipment.** Most pools have buoys, kickboards, and other swim aids available for use. Before using one of these, ask a lifeguard for permission. If there is equipment at the end of a lane, assume someone else is using it.

FEAR OF WATER

Sometime around 1985 a friend of mine decided to do his first open-water triathlon. It was an Olympic-distance race, with a 1,500-meter swim in a small lake. The race was in Wyoming in the spring, so the water was cold, and we all wore wet suits. Dave was a very good pool swimmer who usually swam about the same pace as I did in workouts. When the race started, Dave was right next to me, but he quickly disappeared. After the race I found him sitting quietly in my car in the parking area. He told me that he had panicked in the first few minutes of the swim and headed straight back to the shore. He was devastated. It looked like the end of his new triathlon lifestyle, and all because of a great fear of open water.

Being a fighter, Dave decided not to throw in the towel but instead embarked on a mission to overcome his fear of open water. It took the better part of a year to accomplish this. During that time he swam in open water whenever he could find someone to go with him. He started by staying close to the shoreline, where he could easily stand up whenever he wanted. Over time he gradually moved away from the shore and learned to navigate using landmarks. He went on to be an excellent triathlete and even qualified for the Hawaii Ironman Triathlon World Championship.

Dave's story is a good example of why you should be respectful of and cautious in open water. Never take it for granted; but also don't accept fear as a normal condition. Imagining all of the things that *could* go wrong only fuels fear.

When you are ready, get started in open-water swimming incrementally. Just as Dave did, stay close to the shore as you develop skills and attitudes. Venture farther out only when you're ready. Always swim with a buddy in open water—never alone even if you're hugging the shoreline. It will take time, but you can overcome your fear of the water.

SWIM STUFF

You don't need much gear to get started in swimming, and the stuff you do need is not very expensive. Obviously you need a swimsuit, and you may already have one. In a triathlon some men swim in a swimmer's Lycra brief-cut suit. A tight-fitting, mid-thigh-length Lycra suit is becoming more popular for men at triathlons and in pools. One nice feature of this type of short is that you can swim, bike, and run in it. These long-leg swimsuits also have a small crotch pad for cycling. These are best used only during the race, not in swim training.

You could wear a loose-fitting swimsuit like the one you wear when you go to the beach. You will see plenty of these in your first triathlon and at the pool. The problem with baggy swimsuits is that they slow you down a lot because of the drag they create both in the water and on the bike, and this drag will make learning good swim technique a bit more difficult.

I understand men's reluctance to wear form-fitting Lycra in public; it definitely takes some getting used to. For now, as you get started swimming, a baggy suit will do, but observe what others at the pool are wearing, especially the triathletes. Then when you feel ready, shop around for a mid-thigh-length swimsuit. Many men wear a loose-fitting pair of shorts, like running shorts, over their long-leg suit as they go to and from the locker room at the pool, taking them off just before they get in the water.

For women the traditional one-piece Lycra swimsuit is common at the pool and at triathlons. In the race you will see some women in one-piece Lycra and spandex "skinsuits." These are sleeveless, round-neck tops fastened to a thigh-length, form-fitting short with a small crotch pad for biking. Another option for the race is separate tops and bottoms made like the skinsuit. Some women wear briefer shorts and tops to reduce drag in the water. As a newbie there is no reason for you to be concerned with going really fast. The standard, one-piece Lycra swimsuit that you probably already have will work fine for the race and the pool. After the swim in the triathlon you can always pull on a pair of bike shorts.

In Chapter 10 I tell you more about what to wear in your first triathlon, so here we're just concerned with what to wear at the pool. If you have to buy something, men's swimsuits run about $30 to $50. Women's swimwear costs a little more, around $50 to $75. One-piece skinsuits start at around $90. Separate tops and bottoms cost in the neighborhood of $40 to $60 each.

The only other equipment you need is goggles. Finding the right pair can be tricky, because a waterproof fit and comfort are the main concerns. You won't really be able to tell if the goggles are right until you give them a try during a swim. However, to get an idea at the store, you can place the goggles on your face without putting the strap around your head. If the goggles are waterproof you should be able to push the eyepieces against your face and feel the suction hold them in place for a couple of seconds. If they won't stay in place even for a second, then they aren't right for you. Once you've narrowed down the selection, try the finalists on with the strap around your head to see if they feel comfortable. There should be no pressure on the bridge of your nose, and they should feel as if they would stay in place even if someone bumped against you while swimming.

Two basic types of goggles are used in triathlon: the two-piece type, with separate eye lenses connected by a soft, flexible nose piece, and the one-piece kind, similar to what scuba divers wear, only smaller. Expect to pay anywhere from $7 to $50.

Depending on your personal preference, you may also want to get a nose clip and earplugs. These can be picked up inexpensively in a general sporting goods store or at a swim specialty shop. It's also a good idea to have a spare pair of swim goggles for the triathlon—just in case. But don't buy these until you are certain of the best type for your face. There are lots of other swim aids used in the pool, such as fins, kickboards, pull buoys, and other learning tools. The pool you swim at is likely to have most of these on hand, so there is no reason to buy them now. Later on you may want to consider something along this line to work on technique.

Notice that I didn't mention buying a wet suit. If you follow triathlon, you may be aware that in many races wet suits are worn in the swim because the open water is cold. As mentioned earlier, I wouldn't recommend an open-water swim for your first triathlon—warm or cold water. In Chapter 11 I tell you how to go about choosing a race. Should you decide to do a triathlon with a cold open-water swim, I recommend renting a wet suit at a triathlon, swim, bike, or run store. If you go this route be sure to reserve it weeks in advance or you may be beaten out by others. Later, once the triathlon bug has bitten you, you can look into buying your own wet suit. This is a very technical purchase, so having more experience is helpful.

Chapter 6

YOUR BIKING

You won't cover much real estate when running and even less when swimming, but you can see a lot in an hour or so of bike riding. You'll get to know the details of the roads and bike paths where you ride better than you ever have in your car or on foot. In a car you are insulated from the rest of the world, which goes by quickly. When walking or running, your range is pretty small. But on a bike you experience the world firsthand and travel many miles.

Many experienced triathletes consider the bike leg of a triathlon the most important because they spend about half the total race time on two wheels. In comparison with the swim and run, the bike involves the most technology, as it's the only part of a triathlon done on a machine. And since you are dealing with technology, this is also the most expensive part of getting equipped for your first triathlon.

DUSTING OFF THE OLD BIKE

You don't have to ride a fancy, expensive bike to do your first triathlon. In fact, I recommend using whatever bike you already have in the garage, as long as it's safe to ride. If you're unsure about that, take it to a local bike shop and have the mechanic take a look. If you've chosen a first-timer-friendly race, you'll find lots of people riding all kinds of bikes, many of which are in disrepair. But be sure to have yours fixed up a bit. You don't want it breaking down on a long ride far from home.

Schedule your trusty steed for a tune-up. If your bike has been sitting around gathering dust it probably needs some maintenance to make it road-ready, including chain lubrication, brake and tire pad replacement, and adjustment of all cables, bolts, and bearing races. After the tune-up you'll be surprised at how much easier—and fun!—it is to ride.

BUYING A BIKE

But what if you're in the mood to buy a new bike? Again, I don't recommend doing this. Buying a bike is a tricky venture even for a seasoned triathlete. Once you have a couple of races under your belt, you'll have a much better idea what you need in a bike. And chances are that if you do buy a new bike now, after you know more you will regret having purchased it.

Okay, I couldn't convince you, and you are determined to spend some money. So what do you buy? First decide what category of bike to purchase. There are five major categories, and each has good and bad points. You need to decide if you want a bike that will only be used for triathlons or if you also want to use it for century (100-mile) rides, tours, errands around town, or off-road riding. Tough question, huh? This is why I suggest waiting. Anyway, here are your choices.

Triathlon Bike

If you know you're going to use the bike primarily for triathlons, which you will do several of, with maybe an occasional century or short tour, then this is the way to go. Triathlon bikes are made to help you go fast when riding alone. They are designed for aerodynamics and speed, not comfort. Riding one of these will put you in a low position, with your upper-body weight resting on your elbows. They may not be ridden off-road on trails at all.

The following is a description of the major features of a triathlon bike (see Figure 6.1):

- **Frame (main triangle usually made of tubes).** The upright seat tube is generally steeper (more vertical) than on other bikes to give you a slightly lower and more aerodynamic position.
- **Wheels.** They usually have a diameter of 700 millimeters or 27 inches. They often have a low number of spokes (16 to 32) or have a solid-looking disk wheel in the rear for aerodynamics.
- **Tires.** The tires are narrow and pumped to a very high pressure to give you more speed.
- **Gears.** Two chainrings are common in the front, although you can have a third, smaller one installed for hilly courses. Newer bikes have nine or ten gears on the rear wheel.
- **Handlebars.** On a tri bike the handlebars are low and narrow, with supports to put your elbows on, to reduce the amount of speed-robbing drag your body creates.

FIGURE 6.1 *Triathlon bike*

Road Bike

The road bike was designed for bike racing, as in the Tour de France. It's a bit more versatile than the triathlon bike, allowing you to easily ride in tours, centuries, and even triathlons. Road bikes are more comfortable than most triathlon bikes for rides of long duration. These bikes are very responsive—like a race car—due to their short wheelbase and stiff frame design. So the first time you ride one, you may feel a little nervous about even letting go with one hand to reach for a water bottle.

Following is a description of the major features of a road bike (see Figure 6.2):

- **Frame.** The seat tube is less steep than on a tri bike, helping you to sit more comfortably and climb hills better.
- **Wheels.** As on a triathlon bike, the wheels on a road bike are generally 700 millimeters or 27 inches in diameter. They usually have 32 to 36 spokes.
- **Tires.** The tires are narrow and pumped to a high pressure, but generally don't ride as hard as a tri bike.

FIGURE 6.2 *Road bike*

- **Gears.** Just as on a tri bike, two chainrings are common in the front, but you can add a third, smaller one to make hill climbing easier. Newer bikes have nine to ten gears on the rear wheel. The gearshift levers are usually built into the brake levers.
- **Handlebars.** Most road bikes come with "drop" (curved downward) handlebars, but you can substitute straight handlebars to sit more upright and comfortably. And for a triathlon you can buy clip-on triathlon bars to lower your body and improve aerodynamics.

Touring Bike

The touring bike is much like a road bike, only with a longer wheelbase and heavier design. These bikes are meant to carry packs and heavy loads. If the road bike is a race car, then the touring bike is a station wagon. It is best used in multiday century rides, but just as with the road bike, it can be adapted for triathlon. This bike is comfortable but not designed for off-road use.

FIGURE 6.3 *Touring bike*

The following is a description of the major features of a touring bike (see Figure 6.3):

- **Frame.** The seat tube angle is much like that of the road bike to improve comfort and climbing.
- **Wheels.** Touring bike wheels are a bit more substantial than those of the other two types, with 32 to 36 spokes and heavier, sturdier rims.
- **Tires.** The tires are also wider than on tri or road bikes and may have a bit more tread. The tire pressure may not be as high as the previous two bikes.
- **Gears.** Three chainrings are common, allowing the rider a wider range of options for going up steep hills with a heavy load or for riding comfortably on a flat section of road.
- **Handlebars.** Most touring bikes have drop handlebars, but you can replace them with straight ones if you want to sit straighter. For a triathlon you can use clip-on bars.

Mountain Bike

The mountain bike is the four-wheel drive of bicycles. This bike is intended primarily for trail riding on rugged terrain. Most people find these bikes very comfortable because the tires are softer, and they usually have a suspension system. But they are slow, and even slower on pavement because of their heavy, knobby tires. If your riding doesn't have to be fast and you intend to ride off-road as well as running short errands, then this is a good choice. The mountain bike can be used in a triathlon just as it is. In fact, you will see a number of people riding them at your first triathlon.

The following is a description of the major features of a mountain bike (see Figure 6.4):

- **Frame.** These bikes are a little smaller than road or tri bikes and have a rugged design.

FIGURE 6.4 *Mountain bike*

- **Wheels.** In order to deal with trail riding, the wheels are even sturdier than on touring bikes and are a bit smaller, at about 26 inches or 650 millimeters diameter.
- **Tires.** The knobby tires are the widest of any of these bikes and have heavy knobs on them to improve traction on loose dirt.
- **Gears.** With three chainrings and a wide range of gears on the rear wheel, this bike can climb very steep hills.
- **Handlebars.** Long, straight handlebars allow you to sit upright.

Hybrid Bike

These are the popular "fitness" bikes ridden by many people at triathlons. They are also sometimes called "cross" bikes because they are a cross among road, touring, and mountain bikes. They can be used for errands around town, on smooth and easy trails, and in short triathlons.

The following is a description of the major features of a hybrid bike (see Figure 6.5):

FIGURE 6.5 *Hybrid bike*

- **Frame.** The shape is similar to a road bike, but the rider sits upright as on a mountain bike. A little sturdier than a road bike, it isn't as heavy as a mountain bike.

- **Wheels.** The wheels are like those on a touring bike, with 32 to 36 spokes and sturdy rims.

- **Tires.** The tires are also similar to those on a touring bike.

- **Gears.** Three chainrings are common, allowing the rider a wider range of options for going up steep hills with a heavy load or riding comfortably on a flat section of road.

- **Handlebars.** They are straight, like those on mountain bikes.

BIKE FIT

No matter whether you use your old bike or buy a new one for your first triathlon, it's important that the bike fit you. Riding a bike that is too big or too small will not only be uncomfortable, which means you won't look forward to training on it, but is also unsafe and likely to cause injury, especially to your knees and back. So if you borrow someone else's bike, make sure it is the right size for you. To get a rough idea of proper sizing, stand over the bike with your shoes on. You should have an inch or two of clearance between your crotch and the top tube. Women typically have more difficulty with bike sizing because their torsos are short relative to their leg length when compared with men. Most bikes are made for men's sizing. A shorter handlebar stem may help to shorten the reach for a woman. If unsure about fit, take the bike to a bike shop and get the opinion of an experienced salesperson.

Once you have the right size frame, you need to make sure it is set up properly for you. The best way to do this is with a bike fit specialist—someone who actually spends time with you making adjustments. This can be a bit expensive, but if you decide to step up to a triathlon bike, I highly recommend it. For now we need to get your bike set so that it's about right. When following the bike-fit suggestions below, be sure not to set the seatpost or handlebar stem too high. There is a mark on the handlebars indicating their safe extension limit. Do not exceed that mark.

The steps to help you get your bike set about right are given below. It's best to do this with your bike in a trainer so it is upright, level, and balanced. Ride your bike on the trainer for ten minutes or so to get warmed up and in a comfortable position. Then you're ready to start making adjustments. It's a good idea to have someone help with this.

Step 1. If you are using cleats on your bike shoes, start by positioning them so that the ball of your foot is directly over the pedal spindle.

Step 2. Set the saddle angle so that it is flat or parallel to the ground. Then you need to set saddle height. With your bike shoes on, place your heels on the pedals and slowly turn the cranks backward. At the bottom of the stroke your heels should still be on the pedals, with your knee locked out straight. Adjust your saddle height accordingly. Do not adjust it so high that it exceeds the maximum height mark on the seatpost.

Step 3. Adjust the saddle fore-aft position by dropping a plumb line from the front of your knee. A small weighted object on the end of a string will do this quite nicely. The plumb line should drop within a half inch in front of or behind the pedal spindle without changing your position on the saddle. If you moved the saddle either forward or backward you will need to once again check your fore-aft position with a plumb line.

Step 4. Next, set the handlebar height so it is about 2 to 3 inches below the top of your saddle. Do not raise it so high that it exceeds the maximum height line engraved on the portion of the stem that goes into the head tube.

Step 5. When the handlebar stem is the proper length, the handlebars should keep you from seeing the front hub as you look down. If you are well behind or forward of this position, then either the frame is the wrong size or the stem is not the right length. In either case it's best to take the bike to a bike shop at this time for an evaluation. The staff there can change out the stem for you if necessary.

BIKE STUFF

When you're getting ready for your first triathlon, it's important to have the right gear in all three sports, but you'll find that bicycling requires the most stuff. I like to divide triathlon bike equipment into two categories—must-have and nice-to-have. Let's start with the must-have category. This list, of course, assumes that you have a decent bike that is safe and in good working order.

Helmet

In the old days of triathlon (ca. 1985), helmets were optional. That is no longer true, and with good reason. Safety on the bike should be your paramount concern, but accidents outside of your control can, and do, happen. Race directors now require all participants to wear an approved helmet designed for use on a bicycle. This is one area in which you should not skimp on price. Choose your new helmet based first on head protection and fit and second on color and style.

And then wear it whenever and wherever you ride, no matter how slow or easy you might be going. You never know when you might need it. Helmets run $50 to $200.

Bike Shorts

You're going to spend a lot of time on your saddle as you get ready for your first triathlon. A good pair of bike shorts with a padded crotch pad will help the time go by quickly. Running shorts won't hack it. You need some cushioning between your rear and the saddle. Don't wear underwear beneath them, as that defeats the purpose. Most bike shorts are black because you might have to wipe your greasy hands on them during a ride. There are two main

Running shorts won't hack it. You need some cushioning between your rear and the saddle.

types to choose from: loose-fitting, touring-style shorts, and tight-fitting racer shorts. Either will work fine for your first triathlon, so your choice comes down to style and preference. Expect to pay $35 to $200 for shorts.

Pumps

You'll need two pumps—one for your bike (a frame pump) and a floor pump. The frame pump is carried while you ride in case of a flat out on the road. The first time you have to use it you'll understand why I say also buy a floor pump. It's common to have to pump your tires every few days before starting a ride. Using a frame pump every time makes this a workout in itself. The floor pump just stays in your garage until needed. An alternative to a frame pump that is popular among triathletes is carrying CO_2 cartridges during a ride. These take up less space and are much easier to use when a tube needs inflating after a flat. Frame pumps cost $10 to $50. CO_2 cartridges go for about $1 apiece. You'll need a device to connect the cartridge to the valve stem. These cost $15 to $30 and include a few cartridges to get you started. Floor pumps cost $20 to $100.

Gloves

Like bike shorts, this is another product that makes riding more comfortable. Padded gloves also protect your hands in case of a fall. And when you get really good at riding a bike, they also can be used to flick stickers and glass off your tires without stopping or cutting your hands. Fingerless gloves are best for road riding in warmer months. Gloves cost anywhere from $13 to $35.

Bottle Cage

You'll want to carry water or a sports drink on your bike both while training and in the race. There are several options for doing this, but the simplest and least expensive is having a bottle cage mounted on your bike. You may already have one of these, but if you don't, look to spend $7 to $40.

Repair Kit

Chances are that someday you will get a flat tire during one of your rides. It could be a long walk home, so carrying the basic needs for repairing a flat, and knowing how to fix it, is a necessity (see the "How to Repair a Flat" sidebar). You can pick up a small patch kit and some tire levers in a bike shop. Also purchase a spare tube and carry it on all rides. This is what you go to first in case of a flat. Should you have a second flat on the same ride, you'll have to use the patch kit to repair it. It's also very helpful to have a small saddlebag that fastens under your seat to carry all of this. In the saddlebag, you can carry a few dollars for an emergency phone call or a sports drink. Altogether, this kit will cost you about $30.

If you had to buy all of the must-haves discussed above (you probably have some of it already), you would spend at least $145. That may seem like a lot, but given that you are making a long-term commitment to triathlon, you should think of it as an investment in your health, fitness, and lifestyle, not a onetime, frivolous expense.

⊙ HOW TO REPAIR A FLAT

You're riding along and become aware that a tire is going flat because the bike seems to be handling differently. Slow leaks, rather than sudden blowouts, are the most common type of flat. Stop riding before the tire is completely out of air and you are riding on the rim only. Here are the steps for getting your tire ready to go again. It's a good idea to practice this a few times in your garage before you are forced to do it 10 miles from home. Of course if you have a bike jersey with pockets in the back, you can carry a cell phone and call someone to pick you up. Then you can repair the flat in the comfort of your garage. But here's how to fix the flat wherever you may be.

1. Remove the wheel from the bike. This is when having quick releases rather than bolts with nuts comes in handy. You will probably have to open the brake calipers at the wheel by pulling up on the small handle on the side. If it's the front wheel, you may need to open the release quite widely, since newer bikes often have safety tabs to prevent the wheel from coming out accidentally. If it's the rear wheel, shift gears so that you are in the small-est cog on the wheel. This will make it easier to reinstall the wheel.

FIGURE 6.6

FIGURE 6.7

FIGURE 6.8

2. Remove only one side of the tire from the rim. Start by making sure all of the air is out of the tire by opening and pressing the inner tube valve (Figure 6.6). Then insert a tire lever under one side of the tire on the opposite side from the valve and pry the tire off (Figures 6.7 and 6.8). Slide the tire lever either forward or backward along the rim to remove more of the tire from the rim. If you can't slide the lever, pry a second part of the tire loose 2 or 3

continued ⊛

How to Repair a Flat *(continued)*

inches from the original spot using the other lever. This will loosen a wider part of the tire, and you should be able to slide a lever and remove one side of the tire all the way around the wheel.

3. Remove the tube. If there is a nut on the valve stem, take it off. Reach under the tire and pull out the tube, removing it entirely from the wheel and tire (Figure 6.9). Maintain the tube's original orientation with the wheel in case you have to figure out where the puncture is.

FIGURE 6.9

4. Find the puncture. There are two types of punctures. One is caused by a sharp object such as a piece of glass or thorn penetrating the tire and tube. By slowly running your fingers around the inside of the tire you can often find and remove this object. The other type is called a "pinch flat" and commonly occurs when the tire is underinflated. If there isn't enough air pressure, when you hit an obstacle such as railroad tracks or a pothole the tube is pinched against both sides of the rim, causing two small holes that look like a snake bite. If you don't find a sharp object, chances are you have a pinch flat, which you can confirm by finding the holes. If they aren't immediately obvious, pump some air into the tube and slowly pass it by your ear, listening for escaping air. If you find two holes there, it was a pinch. If there is only one it was a sharp object puncture. If you kept the tube's orientation with the tire you should now be able to examine the area where the puncture occurred to make sure there is no glass, thorn, or other sharp objects that may puncture the spare tube when it's installed.

If you don't have a spare tube, your only option is to patch the puncture. Using the sandpaper in your patch kit, roughen the area around the puncture. Then apply a thin coat of rubber cement from the patch kit to an area slightly larger than the patch. Allow the cement to dry for several minutes. It is dry when it no longer glistens. Without touching the contact area, remove the patch from the foil and carefully lay

How to Repair a Flat *(continued)*

it on the cemented area. Use your thumbs and fingers to press the patch into place, working from the center of the patch toward the edges. Once it is patched, put a little bit of air into the tube to make sure it holds and check the tube for other punctures.

5. Install the spare or repaired tube. Put just enough air in the spare tube to give it shape. If you are using CO_2 cartridges, rather than risking emptying the cartridge, use your mouth to blow a little air into the tube. Remove the nut, if there is one, from the valve stem. Insert the valve stem into the rim hole first. Then fit the tube into the open side of the tire all the way around.

6. Put the tire back into place on the rim. Start by pushing the valve stem up into the tire casing and allowing it to settle into position on its own (Figure 6.10). Then, starting at the valve stem and using your thumbs, push the tire back into the rim, working away from the valve stem in both directions at the same time. When you get to the last few inches of tire, deflate the tube entirely. This will make it easier to finish it off. Reinstalling the last few inches is the hardest part of the entire project. It's best to do this using only the heels of your hands by rolling the tire bead up and toward the rim (Figure 6.11). If you can't get it to pop into place, carefully use a tire lever to do so, being sure not to pinch the tube against the rim.

FIGURE 6.10

FIGURE 6.11

7. Pump up the tube. Put just enough air in the tube to give it shape and then examine the tire all the way around to make sure no tube is protruding out under the tire. This will cause another flat. Once you are certain the tube is properly inflated, pump it to the pressure rating on the side of the tire. If you're using a hand

continued ➔

How to Repair a Flat *(continued)*

pump you'll have to guess this based on feel. If you're using a CO_2 cartridge, put all of the air into the tube by holding the cartridge handle fully depressed until there is no more gas going into the tube.

8. Replace the wheel on the bike. If it's the front wheel, slip it into place, making sure it is centered between the brake pads, and then screw the quick release or nut back into place. If it's the rear wheel, pull the rear derailleur backward and place the chain on the smallest cog. Let go of the derailleur and slip the wheel into the dropout slots. Center the wheel between the brake pads and tighten the locking mechanism. In either case, be sure to push the lever on the brake caliper down to properly space the brakes from the rim.

Now let's take a look at a few nice-to-haves. These are products that will either make you faster or more comfortable or make training easier. But they are not necessities. Triathletes tend to add these items to their arsenals over time, starting soon after their first race.

Bike Shoes

This one could really be in either category. Once you have your first triathlon behind you, put this on your must-have list. For now you can ride in running shoes, and lots of new triathletes do. But because they are flexible and soft, you not only lose power but your feet can get sore on longer rides. For right now your rides won't be all that long. You have two choices in shoes—road and touring. Road shoes are stiffer, allowing you to transfer more power to the pedals on each stroke. The downside is that they are hard to walk around in should you want to walk a lot. That's generally not the case when training for a triathlon. But if you also want to use the same shoes when doing centuries and tours, then touring shoes may be better since they are a bit more flexible and easier to walk in. Shoes are about $60 to $300.

Aerobars

If you want to race faster in a triathlon, this is the ticket. Aerobars put you into a low, aerodynamic position with your elbows resting on pads and your hands outstretched in front. You can buy either one-piece aerobars or clip-ons that you simply clamp onto your existing handlebars. Aerobars cost $50 to $700.

Special Pedals

Your bike may have come with toe clips. That's the type of pedal that has an adjustable strap that goes around your foot to hold it in place. These work fine, but clipless pedals make stopping at stoplights a breeze. Like ski bindings, you just twist your foot and it pops out. Not necessary, but nice. Expect to pay $50 to $330.

Bike Jersey

You can ride and race in a T-shirt. A lot of people do. But a cotton T-shirt flapping in the breeze will work like a sail to slow you down, and on a hot day it holds a lot of sweat. Bike jerseys resolve those problems and provide pockets in the back to carry stuff like money, a cell phone, spare tube or patch kit, food, facial tissue, or anything else you want to bring along. They are brightly colored to make you easier for motorists to see. Jerseys run $35 to $80.

Special Wheels

Next to having aerobars, special wheels will do the most to make you go fast. You can find some that are solid, called "disk wheels," but I don't recommend those for your first triathlon. Look for those that have thirty-two or fewer spokes to a wheel. The fewer spokes, the less "eggbeater" effect on the air as you travel through it. This means faster speed due to reduced drag. "Fast" wheels can be a big expense and are best left until after your first triathlon. But they are more than likely something you will eventually want. Look to spend anywhere from $200 to $300 or more for a pair of good wheels.

Handlebar Computer

A no-frills handlebar computer tells you current, average, and maximum speed, distance, time, and time of day. Or you can get more bells and whistles, including heart rate, altitude, cadence, grade, night light, temperature, and more. These cost $30 to $300 depending on the number of features.

Indoor Trainer

If you live someplace that is really cold in the winter or really hot in the summer, you may want to consider buying an indoor trainer. This is a small device that you mount your bike on. It provides resistance against the rear wheel so that the effort is very much like being out on the open road. It uses a small fan, a magnet, or encased fluid to create the resistance. Trainers allow you to get a ride in when the weather, traffic, darkness, babysitting, or even a good show on TV wouldn't otherwise allow it. Trainers cost $130 to $550.

Trainers allow you to get a ride in when the weather, traffic, darkness, babysitting, or even a good show on TV wouldn't otherwise allow it.

Mirror

If you will spend a lot of time riding your bike on public streets and roads, having a mirror will help you ride more safely and provide some peace of mind about what is coming up behind you. With a mirror you can keep your eye on traffic without turning your head, which can be tricky at times, and also see others riding behind you. Mirrors fasten either to your helmet or to the end of your handlebars. They cost $5 to $20.

HOW TO RIDE A BIKE

Believe it or not, there are right and wrong ways to sit on a bike. The wrong way is like sitting on a bar stool and leaning on the bar. Your back is arched like a cat's back instead of being straight. That restricts breathing slightly, making it harder to breathe while pedaling the bike. To get your back right, you need to first get your pelvis right. Think of your pelvis as a bowl filled with water. In the bar stool sitting position no water spills out of the bowl because it is level on all sides. Although that may sound comfortable, besides curving your back, it also means that the big muscles of your thighs—the hamstrings and quads—are restricted and unable to fully deliver power to the pedals. You don't want to ride a bike this way.

So how should you sit? Again, going back to your pelvis as a bowl, sit so that the water spills out of the front side. This means your pelvis is slightly tilted, with the front part of the bowl lower than the rear part. Sitting this way takes some practice and getting used to, but once you get it you will have a flatter back, allowing you to move more air in and out of your lungs, and your leg muscles will work more effectively.

You may find that sitting on the bike this way causes some groin discomfort. That's a sign that either your saddle isn't right for you or that the bike isn't set up properly, or both. Having your bike properly set up by a fit specialist will make it easier to sit this way.

Pedaling a bike seems fairly simple also. After all, your feet are on pedals, which are attached to crankarms revolving around a fixed point at the bottom bracket. What could go wrong? Actually, quite a bit. Sports scientists have shown that there are differences in pedaling ability among even experienced athletes. These differences mean that some riders are more efficient than others. Those who pedal most smoothly gain their efficiency primarily at the top and bottom of the pedal circle. Learning to pedal more like them means you can go faster with the same effort or that you can ride easier at the same speed.

Anyone can push down on the pedal correctly because the way we are built and gravity combine to make the pedal go from top to bottom easily. The tricky parts are the top and bottom of the stroke. These are a bit more difficult to get right, but if you do, riding will be a whole lot more fun. So let's figure out the top and bottom parts of the pedal stroke.

The reason the top and bottom are so tricky has to do with changes in direction. As the foot and pedal are approaching the top of the stroke, the leg has to change direction, from going back and up to forward and down. As it approaches the bottom of the stroke, the opposite has to happen. These changes, or "transitions," are difficult to get right, especially the top one. Do them wrong and you waste energy—something you can't afford to do when riding hard in a triathlon.

So how do you make the transitions smooth? Watch your foot position on the pedal and train your muscles. When pedaling, your heel should be slightly (about half an inch) higher than the ball of your foot. This angles your foot just enough so that the transitions are easier. To train your muscles to work correctly, do drills.

Drills

You can incorporate these drills into the start of every ride for the first few minutes while you're warming up. These concentrate mostly on the top transition, because it is the more difficult.

Isolated Leg-Training Drill

This is best done on an indoor trainer because it's a bit risky on the road. Unclip one foot from the pedal and place it on a chair or box next to the bike. Then, with the bike in a low and easy gear, pedal with the other leg. You'll find that at the top of the pedal stroke there is a "dead" spot that is a bit difficult to pedal through. Focus on this dead spot to smooth it out. At first you will last only a few seconds with one leg, as it fatigues quickly. Change legs when this happens. Over time you will become more efficient at the top of the stroke and be able to pedal longer before tiring. This is a sign that your transitions are improving.

9-to-3 Drill

This and all of the following drills are done with both feet clipped into the pedals and may be used on the road or indoor trainer. In the 9-to-3 drill, think of the pedal stroke as being the face of a clock, with 12 o'clock at the top and 6 o'clock at the bottom. When the crankarms are parallel to the ground, the forward foot is in the 3 o'clock position and the back foot is at 9 o'clock. What you want to do in this drill is feel like you are moving your rear foot straight forward from 9 to 3 on the clock face without ever going through 12. Obviously you are, but by firing the muscles this way you train them to transition smoothly. Every minute or so, think about pedaling this way for several seconds. Take a mental break and then do it again. Repeat this frequently throughout the ride, especially in the early part during warm-up.

> What you want to do in this drill is feel like you are moving your rear foot straight forward from 9 to 3 on the clock face without ever going through 12.

Shoe Top Drill

This one is a bit challenging, but great for getting the transitions right. As you are pedaling, try to keep your foot against the top inside of your shoe and avoid touching the bottom inside of your shoe. This drill emphasizes all parts of the pedal stroke except the downstroke, which is the easy part.

Toe-Touch Drill

The toe-touch drill causes you to focus more on the top transition. As your foot approaches the 12 o'clock position, try to touch your toes to the front end of your shoe. Make sure your heel is slightly higher than the ball of your foot when doing this.

Spin-Up Drill

Cadence, how many pedal strokes one foot completes in a minute, has a lot to do with how efficiently you pedal. Each of us has a comfortable cadence range. When your cadence falls below your comfortable range, you feel like you are using too much muscle to push down. When it is higher than your comfortable range, you begin breathing too hard for how fast you are going. Efficient riders tend to have higher comfort ranges than inefficient riders. The spin-up drill helps to raise your comfort range by making you more efficient, with a faster cadence. The drill is easy. Gradually increase your cadence for about 20 to 30 seconds until you start to bounce on the saddle. Then reduce your cadence slightly until you stop bouncing, and pedal as smoothly as you can for a few seconds. Repeat this drill several times early in a ride during the warm-up. Over time your comfortable range will move up.

Shifting Gears

Your comfort range also has a lot to do with shifting gears. As I mentioned in the spin-up drill section, when your cadence is above or below your natural comfort range, you feel like you are either using too much muscle (very low cadence) or are breathing too hard (very high cadence). Shifting gears allows you to keep the balance between muscle and breathing as comfortable as possible. If you feel like you are working too hard, try shifting to either a higher or a lower gear to see if that helps. Sometimes it does. But when you are riding as hard as you can, all you can do is find the best gearing combination. The hard work of riding fast is going to make you uncomfortable regardless.

You'll hear the phrases "high gear" and "low gear" a lot in bicycling. A high gear is one that slows your cadence down and causes you to rely more heavily on muscle to turn the cranks. A low gear does just the opposite—it raises your cadence, making you breathe harder. When riding you always want to find the best gear for the current conditions—hills, wind, and how fresh you are feeling. As I mentioned, just shifting to a higher or lower gear sometimes makes the effort feel easier.

The highest gears use the big chainring, while the lowest gears use the small chainring. The gear cluster on the rear wheel works in just the opposite way. The bigger the gear, the easier it is to turn the pedals, and the smaller the gear, the harder it is to turn them. So by combining big or small chainrings with bigger or smaller gears on the rear wheel, you can create many different combinations to fine-tune the effort you put out while pedaling.

There are a couple of combinations you won't want to use, however. It's best not to use the big chainring with the largest gear on the back wheel, the one closest to the spokes. Nor should you combine the small chainring with the smallest gear on the rear wheel, the one farthest from the spokes. These gearing combinations are called "crossover," meaning that the chain is running at an extreme angle from front to back. This increases the wear and tear on the chain and gears, causing them to need replacing sooner.

BIKE SAFETY

This is the part where I say "don't" a lot. I'll start by saying, don't take safety for granted. You want to have fun and become a better person because of triathlon. A crash can stop that in a heartbeat. Safety, safety, safety!

Riding a bike on the open road with traffic is scary—and with good reason. It's a bit like being a mouse in an elephant stampede. Almost every week I hear of a cyclist who has a bad accident, the worst of which are bike-car accidents. The most common reason for these is inattentiveness of either the bike rider or the driver—or both. You have no control over drivers, but when in or near traffic *you* must always be attentive. Don't assume the drivers are. In fact, assume they aren't and that they don't even see you. Chances are you will be right.

Never take needless risks on the road. It is better to stop fully (with a foot on the ground) while watching to see what drivers are going to do at an intersection than to bolt through it to keep your workout going. Always ride with your eyes looking ahead and scanning the area around you, not down at your front wheel because of fatigue or a determination to ride faster. You need to know what's just up the road and what drivers and other riders are doing. Don't become a statistic for the sake of fitness. All it takes is a second of inattentiveness.

> **Always ride with your eyes looking ahead and scanning the area around you, not down at your front wheel because of fatigue or a determination to ride faster.**

Although bike-car accidents are usually the most devastating, they are not the most common. Falls account for perhaps half of all bike accidents. The next big category is bicycle-bicycle collisions. Dogs, obstacles, and other causes make up the remainder. Most of these are under your control: choose your course wisely, ride defensively, have good skills, make sure your bike is road-ready, and be attentive to what's going on around you.

Equipment Safety

Always wear a helmet. Enough said.

A common cause of accidents is not having the wheels securely fastened to the bike. A wheel wobbling in the frame and coming loose on a descent could be catastrophic. If your wheels lock on with bolts, make sure the nuts are tight. If you have quick-release skewers, it should take quite a bit of effort to close the lever all the way.

Be sure that your tires are fully inflated before every ride. Check the tread to make sure there isn't a small piece of glass or wire stuck in it. Look to see if the thread is showing on your tires. If it is, replace them immediately. If your tires are old from sitting in the garage for a long time, they may be cracked and should be replaced. There should be no bulges in the sidewall.

Check your brakes frequently. The levers should not touch the handlebars. If they do, have a mechanic adjust them. The brake pads should touch the metal wheel rims, not the tires. If they touch the tires even a little bit, the tire will blow out. Replace the brake pads when the vertical wear lines are worn off.

Lean heavily on your handlebar ends before starting a ride to make sure they don't slip. They should be very securely fastened to the stem. There should be plugs on the ends of your bars.

Seeing and Being Seen

Since you want to be seen by drivers, wear bright clothing. Gray or brown clothing is not generally the best choice. It helps to have a mirror either on your helmet or on the handlebars. However, you will still have blind spots and need to check them before changing lanes or turning. Riding at dusk or dawn is not recommended, but a lot of triathletes do this, especially in the winter when daylight is limited, in order to get in their training miles. Bright headlights, taillights, and reflectors are necessities at these times. Riding indoors on a trainer is much safer.

Choosing a Safe Course

Always remember that riding a bike is a lot different than driving a car. This is most evident when you're deciding where to ride. It's best to avoid riding on busy streets, at rush hour, in the dark, on streets that have no bike lanes, and against traffic on one-way streets. The safest places to ride are usually bike paths and wide roads with little traffic. As you drive around in your car, make a mental note of the best places to ride. Then plan your routes accordingly. At certain times of the day it may be best not to ride outside at all due to traffic, darkness, or foul weather. This is when having an indoor trainer (see "Bike Stuff" in this chapter) comes in very handy.

Scout two types of safe bike courses you can ride. Some of the courses should be fairly flat—as flat as you can find where you live. These will be used on days when you want to keep it easy, develop a good base of aerobic fitness, or work on race-type riding. Also have a hilly course or two, ones with grades that challenge you a bit just to get over them. Later in your training we will use these to make you stronger.

Stay to the Right

Always ride to the side of the road in the same direction traffic is flowing. Don't ride on the sidewalk. Stay about 12 to 18 inches left of the edge of the road. This may seem counterintuitive, but hugging the edge encourages drivers, especially on narrow roads, to squeeze between you and oncoming traffic. If you stay well to the left of the edge, they are more likely to wait for a safer moment to pass, and you have room to maneuver.

Parked cars present a unique problem when riding on the right side. Check to see which cars have people in them who may open the door at the last second. Give these cars a wide berth after checking traffic over your left shoulder. If you're unsure, give a car a bit of extra space regardless. Don't weave in and out of parked cars, as drivers behind you may not see you or may misunderstand your intent.

Holding Your Line

Try to always ride in a predictable manner. This generally means holding a straight line. That way riders behind you and drivers are relatively sure of your intent. Never ride "no hands." Have at least one hand on the handlebars at all times. Learn where your water bottle on the frame is located so you don't have to take your eyes off the road to grab it. Same goes for putting it back in the cage; a quick glance is all it should take.

Looking over Your Shoulder

Perhaps the trickiest move for all riders, including very experienced ones, is looking over their left shoulder to check traffic when turning or changing lanes. The bike will often start drifting left when a rider does this. One way to avoid this is to lock your left elbow and slightly bend your right elbow. That way the bike stays on a straight course. A mirror will help to eliminate a lot of this turning. You'll still need to turn your head for a final check before moving left, however.

Hand Signals

It's always a good idea to let others know you are turning by using hand signals. This helps drivers and others riding with you to know what to expect. Commonly accepted hand signals follow:

- **Stopping.** Left arm extended down with hand open and palm facing backward.
- **Left turn.** Left arm extended and pointing left.
- **Right turn.** This one varies a bit from state to state. For drivers in all states and cyclists in most, the left elbow is bent with the hand pointing straight up. In other states cyclists can simply point right with an extended right arm.

Cornering and Turning

One of the most dangerous occurrences during a bicycle ride, especially a fast one, is negotiating corners.

The first rule of cornering is, don't brake in the corner. If the turn is free of gravel and water you should be able to take it at full speed by leaning. But if it's necessary to slow down, brake before you get into the turn. Then let go of the brake levers as the turn begins.

The most important moment in taking a corner safely is the early part. If the speed and line you selected are right, you will have no problems. Practice approaching corners at various speeds. Make it second nature to judge how fast to take them. The line you select depends on speed. A fast speed requires a more gradual and sweeping turn than does slow cornering.

Sit in the middle of your saddle, not on the nose or back end of it. This will help you maintain balance. As the turn starts, stop pedaling so that your inside knee is high, put most of your weight on the outside pedal, and lean to the inside. The faster you are going, the more you should lean. The lean of the bike should be greater than the lean of your upper body. To accomplish this, keep your head upright so that the line of your eyes is parallel to the road surface. Don't lean your head into the turn. When the bike becomes more upright as you exit the corner, begin to pedal again.

Hone your cornering skills by going to a parking lot or other area with no traffic and practicing both left and right turns until you become comfortable with both. Right turns are simple. Signal your intention before arriving at the corner. Check for pedestrians who might step out in front of you. Then stay to the right but away from the very edge of the road as you make the turn. Left turns are a lot trickier. If the street you are on has a dedicated left-turn lane, check traffic approaching from behind, signal you are going left, and then move to the right side of the left-turn lane. Cross when traffic clears and the light is green. For a multi-lane street with no dedicated left-turn lane, stop on the right side and wait for a break in traffic before crossing. Or make a 90-degree turn by riding straight across the intersection to the far corner. Stop to check traffic on the street you were on and then cross the intersection so you are proceeding in the desired direction.

Obstacles

You are bound to encounter obstacles in the bike lane or on the bike path. These can cause falls and flat tires. If you're unsure about whether you can negotiate a large obstruction, it's best to stop, get off the bike, and walk around it. For smaller ones you can make slight changes in your course to avoid them. If you're riding with a group, be sure to point at any obstacles on the course to warn trailing riders.

When approaching railroad tracks that intersect the street at greater or less than a 90-degree angle, alter your course so you cross the tracks at close to a right angle to prevent getting your front wheel twisted. Also, as you cross railroad tracks or very rough sections of road, stand on your pedals with your knees and elbows slightly bent. This will reduce the shock to your body and the bike and also help prevent pinch flats.

Dogs

Chasing dogs will usually leave you alone as soon as you are past their "territory." It's best to pedal fast in a straight line, with both hands on the handlebars, rather than to try to hit the dog with a frame pump or squirt it with a water bottle. You might also try shouting "*Sit!*" since the dog may be trained to obey that command.

Stop Signs and Stoplights

Don't assume you have the right of way even if the light is green. Make sure all cars that could intersect your path are stopped before crossing the street. Be patient. Stop-and-go lights that are controlled by sensors don't "see" bicycles. You must either wait for a car to trip the sensor or get off your bike and press the pedestrian crosswalk button.

Braking and Stopping

The rear brake is operated with the right hand and the front brake with the left hand. The front brake has more stopping power than the rear, but used alone in an emergency situation it may cause you to flip over the handlebars. The rear brake is best for slowing you down gradually and should always be used in conjunction with the front brake. Apply the rear brake to gradually slow the bike, and then the front brake when it's time to stop.

GROUP RIDING

Riding on the roads with a group makes it even more fun to be out on your bike. But before going out with a group, make sure you know how fast they ride and what their purpose is. Some groups are for racers, and they ride fast and aggressively. It's best to avoid this type. Others are more social; they ride slower with possibly even coffee or breakfast stops. There may even be triathletes who ride together, including those who are new to the sport and want to learn more. Your bike shop can tell you more about the groups in your area and suggest the best one for you.

Riding in a group, although fun, can be dangerous. Large groups that dominate the roadway and disobey stop signs tend to make drivers angry and impatient. That's not a good combination. You also need to be more attentive to what's going on around you—such as traffic and obstacles—because you can't see as much. On the other hand, a well-led and disciplined group can make riding safer than when alone since you are easier for drivers to see.

You can also learn a lot from riding with experienced cyclists, including tips for training and racing and bike handling, and updates on the local triathlon scene. This is your chance to meet others with common interests and to become a better rider.

HILLS—UPS AND DOWNS

There's no doubt that riding up hills will make you a stronger bike rider. While riding on a flat stretch of road, you can ease up anytime. But when climbing a hill, letting up may cause you to fall over. You have to reach down deep to find the power to keep going on steep hills. Although they are hard and perhaps even frustrating at first, hills will soon become your strongest ally in the quest to become a better rider.

On hills the trick is to find the right gear combination. New riders tend to select a high gear, stand, and "muscle" the bike up the hill. This puts a lot of stress on the knees and can result in injury. Try to find a gearing combination that allows you to stay seated and spin with a bit higher cadence. It may help to have your bike shop put a third chainring on your bicycle if you find getting over hills is extremely difficult. There is also a new option, called compact chainrings, that gives you lower gears. As you approach a hill, allow your momentum to carry you up a few yards. Then shift quickly to a lower gear. Using the right one for you on any given hill will soon become second nature. But at first you'll need to experiment a bit.

Your position on the bike when going up a hill is a bit different than when riding on flat roads. If you have triathlon aerobars or road drop/hooked bars, place your hands on the top portion of the handlebars near the stem. Although this will make you less aerodynamic, it will give you more power. Wind resistance is less important than power on a hill. It may also help to scoot your rear a little farther back on the saddle so you can push a bit forward with the pedals rather than straight down. Again, this makes you more powerful.

Descending a steep hill can be scary even for the most experienced bike riders. As your bike handling skills get better you'll find that your speed on descents increases. But at first it's okay to gently "feather" the rear brake when it feels like you're starting to go too fast. There is no fitness to be gained from coming down a hill, but there is a lot to be lost. So sit up to break the wind, hold a straight line, concentrate on where you want to go, keep your hands on the brake levers, feather the brakes a bit, and be conservative.

Chapter 7

YOUR RUNNING

The third leg of your first triathlon—the run—is often the most challenging for new triathletes. To fully develop the fitness necessary to run three miles nonstop may take several months, rather than just a few weeks as we are planning to do here. So if you are brand new to running, your goal for the run part of the triathlon will be to finish it vertically with a smile on your face. We don't care how long it takes or how much you may walk. In fact, we will plan on walking and will train for doing it that way. So, no worries, mate!

If you are an experienced runner, your run mileage will drop as you begin to include swimming and biking in your weekly routine. Don't let that bother you. You'll keep the harder run days and use the swim and bike as "recovery" days. You may well run faster (and have fewer injuries) as a result.

RUNNING AND WALKING

If you've looked ahead to Chapter 9 and Appendix D, you may have noticed there is a lot of walking scheduled for the triathlete who is new to running. That's to help prevent the soreness that almost always comes with starting to run for the first time. Walking is a lot easier on your legs and yet will still produce fitness gains for the beginner.

The running schedule in Chapter 9 also calls for interval training right from the start. Running authorities usually frown on this for novices, but my experience has shown that newbies make greater gains when the exercise session is broken into alternating walk and run periods. At first the run portions will be short, with long walk breaks, but soon the walking gets shorter as the run duration is extended. The key here is for you to pay attention to how your legs feel. If the soreness persists for more than forty-eight hours after running, you weren't ready for it. Return to walking only in this situation.

Another way to reduce the risk of soreness is to learn to run using proper form. Unfortunately, most people do not know how to run. In some cases they have even been instructed to run incorrectly by "experts." The quickest way to learn to run using proper form is to run barefoot on grass. Go to a park, pick out a flat or slightly downhill stretch of grass that is about 100 yards long, and inspect it to make sure it is free of debris such as broken glass, animal droppings, and thorns. Then take off your shoes and run quickly over your grassy course. Turn and walk back to where you began. Repeat this three to five more times. This workout is called "strides." (See Workout #8 in Appendix D.)

What you will find when running shoeless is that your running changes in two small but very significant ways. The first noticeable change is that you don't land on your heels; you land with the foot more or less "flat" on the ground with the weight toward the ball of your foot. The other difference is that because you are landing on a flat foot instead of on your heel, you will take more steps to cover the distance than with shoes on—and you'll be faster as a result.

So why does your form change so much when you take your shoes off? The design of running shoes, with a high, padded heel, encourages you to land on the back end of your foot. It just seems logical with so much rubber there. The high heel also makes it difficult to place your foot flat without the aft end touching first. Landing on your heel means you must roll forward over the entire length of your foot—from the heel to the ball—before pushing off for the next stride. The longer the foot is in contact with the ground, the slower you run. Fast runners spend very little time on the ground when compared with back of the packers. They put their feet down and immediately spring off them. In fact, when you land with a flat foot and your weight toward the forefoot, a natural recoil effect is created in your calf muscle. This quickly captures and releases the "potential" energy, springing you up and forward and thus saving some "biological" energy, mostly carbohydrates, a scarce energy source.

The trick is to figure out how to transfer your natural barefoot running form to fully shod running, which is certainly what you will do in your first triathlon. This takes some dedicated practice. Every time you go for a run-walk workout (with shoes on), use the feel of the barefoot technique you experienced on grass. This will take concentration the first several times, but that should not be hard given that the first several runs are quite short in the training plan.

If you have been running for some time and are already well-established as a heel striker, the change will be more difficult. For the experienced runner, there are more strides workouts on grass in the plan. At first these should be the only run workouts in which you use the barefoot technique. But after four of these you should be ready to use the proper form in the first ten minutes of each run before returning to your old form. Over time increase the duration of the barefoot technique. At the first sign of calf, Achilles, or foot problems, reduce the amount of good-form running you do. It may take longer for the experienced runner to change form than it does for the complete beginner, but give it a try. I think you will find that flat-footed landing ultimately makes running easier.

GROUP RUNNING

Should you run with a group or by yourself? There are advantages and disadvantages either way. If you have a hard time getting out the door to start a run, then a small group is for you. Knowing friends are waiting for you is generally all it takes to get those running shoes on. Be careful of joining groups that like to make training runs into mini-races. These groups will push you to go too fast and might soon cause you to break down in some way. For now your run workouts should be quite easy. Look for others who share that point of view.

The best groups are generally those organized weekly by running clubs, running stores, or health clubs. These will often break up the crowd into smaller groups by ability, scout out a safe course, and may even provide sports drinks along the way. Ask around to find a group that is right for you. You may need to make some changes to the suggested training plan in Chapter 9 to fit into the group. That's okay.

STAYING HEALTHY

If you're going to get injured in triathlon it is likely to be from running. The reason for this is the stress placed on your legs by pounding the pavement. Also, when running your leg muscles are used differently than in the other two sports. The big muscles of the legs—for example, the thigh and calf—lengthen at the same time they are trying to shorten during the running stride. Sports scientists call this "eccentric contraction." Because of the pounding and eccentric contractions, runners have a high likelihood of injury.

For a triathlete, nothing is worse than an injury. Not only is there discomfort, but there is also a feeling of frustration as hard-earned fitness erodes while you sit around waiting for the injury to heal. Those new to running are likely to experience sore knees, shin and foot discomfort, and other aches and pains. Among the worst injuries for runners are stress fractures, patellar tendonitis, patellofemoral syndrome, plantar fascitis, and iliotibial band syndrome.

There are typically four causes of running injuries. The first is poor technique, addressed previously in this chapter. But your technique may also be related to a second cause—weakness or inflexibility. It takes at least several months for the muscles of the legs to adapt to the proper technique. During this adjustment period all of the leg muscles, both the large and small ones, along with tendons and bones, are going through change. There are also adaptations taking place in the upper body from the hips through the entire back. You can't rush these changes. They just take time.

A third cause of injury is running in improper shoes. Later in this chapter I tell you how to go about finding the right shoes, but for now the message is this: Don't run in basketball, aerobics, gym, or any other type of shoe not designed for running. Get the proper equipment for the sport. You'll progress faster and have a much lower risk of injury.

A fourth common cause of running injuries is inherited traits such as flat feet or leg-length differences. Flat feet are quite common and are likely to require a special type of shoe or even an orthotic device (discussed later in this chapter). How do you know if you have flat feet? Look at your footprint on the tile floor after you step out of the shower. If you can see that your arch touched the floor, leaving a "bear paw" impression, then you have flat feet. Other, less common foot problems may also promote injury. It's best to see a sports medicine doctor or podiatrist if you suspect you may have one. You may need orthotics—specially made insoles that help correct imbalances.

> **Don't run in basketball, aerobics, gym, or any other type of shoe not designed for running. Get the proper equipment for the sport. You'll progress faster and have a much lower risk of injury.**

The same is true for leg-length differences. If you keep getting injured in one leg, your legs may be significantly different in length. This sets you up for a unique set of stresses. It's best to see a medical professional, including a physical therapist, if this is the case.

Running on hard surfaces may complicate any of these causes. Excessive training and not enough rest are often the "final straw" that produces the injury. That's why the suggested training schedules in Chapter 9 have you start off so easy with running—I don't want you to get injured.

The best way to deal with injuries, regardless of type, is to prevent them. Proper technique, softer surfaces, good equipment, gradual training increases, stretching, and muscular strength provide the best safeguards. Adequate recovery time following workouts, as prescribed in Chapter 9, is also necessary to stay injury-free.

If all of this fails and tenderness appears, take immediate action. At the first sign of soreness during a workout, stop and walk home. Don't push through unusual discomfort thinking it will go away by itself. Pain is your body's way of telling you "too much."

Should a suspected injury occur, here are the steps to take:

Step 1. Rest the injured area. Stay off of it as much as you can. Don't try to stretch it for at least the first twenty-four hours or test its condition with even limited activity.

Step 2. Apply ice immediately. This can be done with an ice pack (bags of frozen corn make great ice packs) or water frozen in a foam cup (if using the cup, massage the area gently). In either case, apply the ice for about fifteen minutes at a time. If using an ice bag, place a washcloth over the skin to prevent frostbite.

Step 3. Compress it. With some types of injury, such as a sprained ankle, wrapping an elastic bandage around the area snugly will help to control swelling. Be careful not to cut off circulation. If there is noticeable swelling, see your doctor immediately.

Step 4. Elevate it. Keep the injured area above your heart as much as possible. This helps to control swelling.

If the injury doesn't respond to such treatment in the first five days even though you've stopped running, it's time to see your doctor. For some injuries you may be referred to a specialist, such as a podiatrist, orthopedist, or physical therapist.

WHERE TO RUN

One of the best ways to avoid injuries is to run on softer surfaces such as gravel roads, the dirt shoulders of paved roads, running tracks, dirt trails, and grass. These surfaces will absorb some of the impact so it doesn't wreak havoc with your joints. If you must run on pavement, select asphalt over concrete. Even though it's a hard surface, asphalt is softer than concrete.

Also be careful running on terrain that is always sloping in the same direction, either to your left or right. This is common when running in the street facing traffic, with the gutter on your left. Sidewalks also generally have a slight cant sloping downward toward the street. Canted surfaces will put unusual stress on your legs. If you can't avoid side-sloping running routes, at least try to mix them up so you get cants in both directions during a single run. That said, it's best not to run with your back to traffic if in the street.

As your running fitness improves, some of the workouts in Chapter 9 will have you on hills. Running up hills is one of the most effective ways to improve fitness because they force you to work hard. You use more muscle, your heart rate increases, and your breathing becomes faster and more labored. But be careful coming down the other side of the hill, especially if you are on pavement. The pounding of normal running will be greatly magnified but the fitness gains will be minimal. So go slowly on downhills. It's okay to walk.

If possible you should have two types of running courses—a flat one and a hilly one. But what if you live on the coast of Florida or some place similar where there are no hills, or you live in Colorado's Rocky Mountains, where there are no long stretches of flat terrain? One of the best options is treadmill running. Treadmills are also a great alternative when the weather is too nasty to go outside. These running machines allow you to have convenient hills and flats but also give you control over pace, with feedback on how fast you are going. Just be careful not to do all of your running on a treadmill. The repetitive motion without terrain changes due to turns and changing cants can be hard on your legs. It's best to mix up running terrains frequently to give your legs some variety. This is good not only for avoiding injury but also for fitness.

Cars present a real problem for runners. Running next to traffic is one of the most dangerous things you can do in your triathlon training. Yet every day I see people running in the street with their backs to traffic wearing a headset to listen to music or the radio. These people must have a death wish! Never run with your back to traffic, and be extra careful when running outdoors with a headset on. When around traffic be constantly vigilant. Look, listen, and anticipate what drivers might do.

You face many dangerous situations when you run on the streets and roads. One of the most dangerous is approaching an intersection where there is a stopped car waiting for traffic to clear from its left in order to turn right. If you are approaching from the driver's right, chances are good that you will not be seen. Do not enter the intersection until you have made eye contact with the driver or until the car has turned. A third option is to cross the intersection going behind the stopped car. Play it safe when running.

HOT WEATHER

There is no greater stress when exercising than heat, especially when running. To control core temperature when it's hot, the body shunts blood to the skin for cooling before returning it to the heart for pumping to the muscles. This means that the heart must work harder during exercise in the heat, not only to fuel the muscles but also to help with cooling, so your pulse rises. When it comes to choosing between running fast or cooling itself, the body will always select cooling first. Sweating helps to remove heat through evaporation. And since you sweat more on a hot day, the chance of dehydration increases. Following are some tips to help you prepare for the hot days of summer running and doing your first triathlon in the heat:

- **Acclimate.** If you know your first triathlon will be on a hot day, you can help your body get ready. To acclimate to the heat, exercise when the temperature is in the mid-80s or higher for seven or more days in a fourteen-day period. Take it very easy during these workouts.
- **Keep your cool.** In a hot workout or race, pouring cold water on your head and body will lower your body temperature. Put a little ice in your hat or shirt to help lower body temperature.

ⓘ STAYING HYDRATED

Water deprivation has a long history in endurance sports. For example, the Oxford University rowing team of 1860 was restricted to no more than two pints of fluid daily. In 1909, a widely read book on marathon training advised that runners should not drink during a race: "Don't get in the habit of eating and drinking in a marathon race; some prominent runners do, but it is not beneficial."

In the 1920s and 1930s, one of the top runners of the era, Arthur Newton, wrote, "Even in the warmest English weather, a 26-mile run ought to be manageable with no more than a single drink, or at most two."

As late as 1969 endurance athletes were discouraged from drinking water. Some sports even had rules restricting fluid use. The international governing organization for distance running ruled that "refreshments shall (only) be provided by the organizers of a race after 10 miles, and thereafter every 3 miles. No refreshments may be carried or taken by a competitor other than that provided by the organizers."

When I went to college in the 1960s, I can recall thinking what a luxury it was to occasionally have water during practice. In high school, I was taught that athletes must adapt to thirst and dehydration. The reasoning was that it would make us tougher. At the time, my college was "cutting-edge" by allowing small amounts of water. In fact, it wasn't until the 1970s that athletes were encouraged to drink water during workouts and competitions.

Today we know we must avoid, not adapt to, dehydration. For every 2.2 pounds (roughly one quart) of water lost during exercise, heart rate increases by about eight beats per minute, stroke volume—the amount of blood pumped per beat—declines by about one quart per minute, and core temperature rises about a half degree.

During exercise, blood is shunted to the working muscles to supply oxygen and fuel. As blood passes through the muscles, it absorbs heat. To cool the working body,

continued ➔

Staying Hydrated *(continued)*

the warmed blood is transferred to the skin, where some goes into the production of sweat to give off heat. This, combined with fluid losses through heavy breathing, causes a decrease in body fluids. If a 150-pound man loses 2 percent, about 6 cups, of his body weight in water, his running speed or cycling power will decrease by about 10 to 20 percent. A 4 percent loss can produce a 30 percent decline in performance and puts the athlete at risk for heat exhaustion.

To ensure adequate fluid levels, drink at the rate of about 16 to 24 ounces per hour while exercising. For easy exercise lasting less than one hour, water is adequate. For longer workouts or those done in extreme heat, sports drinks are recommended.

Fluid requirements increase during exercise in the heat. To get a rough idea of how much you need to take in, weigh yourself without clothes on before and after a workout. Figure that every pound lost is a pint of water. If you drank during the workout, add one pound for every pint consumed. The remaining deficit is the amount of fluid you need to take in during that type of workout.

- **Use sunscreen.** On a hot, dry day, oil-based sunscreen will block your pores and make conditions worse. Choose a water-based sunscreen instead
- **Age and heat.** Older athletes are more sensitive to the effects of heat than are young athletes. One reason is that sweating tends to decline with aging. Aging competitors also lose more water through urination. The bottom line is that older athletes need to be more scrupulous in taking in fluids than do the youngsters.
- **Use air conditioning.** Using air conditioning at night when you sleep will *not* cause you to lose your heat adaptation. If the heat interrupts your sleep pattern, turn the AC on.

- **Eat for the heat.** Contrary to popular opinion, exercising in the heat causes you to burn more calories than exercising in the cold. So when adapting you may need to increase your calories.

- **Drink for the heat.** Be sure to increase your intake of sports drinks during hot-weather workouts. Aim for 16 to 24 ounces in an hour. Don't drink just plain water for sessions lasting longer than one hour. The rate of absorption of water when compared with a sports drink is about the same.

- **Wipe off sweat.** Frequently wiping the excess sweat from your face, neck, arms, and other body parts while working out will remove oils and accumulated electrolytes, thus allowing your sweat to be more effective at cooling.

RUNNING STUFF

Unlike biking, running is an easy sport to get started in. The only gear you really need is shoes, socks, shorts, and a shirt. Of course, if you go to a running store you will find a lot more stuff, such as hats, water bottle "holsters," special triathlon shoestrings, winter gear, and much more. Some of this, such as winter gear, may be necessary depending on what time of year you're preparing for your first triathlon. But given that getting geared up for the bike can be fairly expensive, I'd suggest purchasing only what you really need for running right now. Here are the basics.

Shoes

This is where almost all of your running budget should go. Running shoes can be expensive depending on how technical they are—and some can be pretty high-tech these days. Whether you should buy the high-tech kind or more basic ones depends on your experience as a runner with injuries and soreness. If you've been running for some time, it's likely that you know what your needs are in these areas. If you are new to running, you can probably start off with more basic—and less expensive—shoes. In either case, I recommend going to a running specialty store to buy shoes. Other stores may be less expensive, but shoes are so complicated these days that you need someone who knows feet, running, and shoes to help you make the right decision. Some types of shoes, including very expensive ones, could actually cause injuries if they're not right for your feet. An experienced salesperson can help you make the right decision by looking at your old shoes (take some old sneakers with you), your feet, and how you look when running with different types of shoes.

Depending on how big you are, what your running form is like, and what kind of surfaces you run on, expect running shoes to last 300 to 500 miles.

Be prepared to spend $75 or more on running shoes. And also understand that they won't last forever. Depending on how big you are, what your running form is like, and what kind of surfaces you run on, expect running shoes to last 300 to 500 miles. That mileage also includes walking around in them. It's best not to use your running shoes for casual wear; save them for running only. When the first pair begins to get old they can be replaced and become your casual shoes.

Socks

Just as with running shoes, socks, and in fact all running clothes, are high-tech these days. With wicking fabrics, mesh weaves, blister prevention, and enhanced durability, these are not your father's gym socks. Again, a running specialty store salesperson can help you match your new shoes with the socks right for you. Expect a pair of socks to cost $6 or more.

Shirt and Shorts

Running shorts usually have a nylon outer shell and a specially designed inner brief that wicks moisture away from the skin while allowing airflow for cooling. They often have small pockets for carrying keys, gel packets, sunglasses, or any other small items you may need. Shorts start at about $30.

Bigger men often have problems with thigh chafing when running. If this proves to be a problem for you, look for a pair of tight-fitting Lycra or spandex shorts to be worn under your running shorts. A lot of triathletes of all sizes and shapes train and race in these shorts exclusively. Some have a small crotch pad built in so they can bike in them also, but I wouldn't recommend doing that except in short races. If chafing during running is all you're trying to prevent, just get a pair of leg-hugging shorts. These can also be used for swimming and cost about $40 or more.

You can do your runs in a T-shirt when the weather is cool, but on hot days or for long runs, cotton won't hack it, because it holds moisture and can chafe. For these runs a loose-mesh shirt made with a wicking fabric is perfect. These are also sold in running stores and start at about $30.

Women should look for tops with built-in support or purchase a sports bra. Support tops cost about $40, and sports bras are about $20. The tops often have a breathable mesh interior panel and T-strap back with a reflective back graphic for visibility in the dark. Many sports bras these days are made to be worn without another top.

Chapter 8

YOUR MUSCLES

Triathlon places a great demand on your aerobic system—your heart, lungs, blood, and aerobic energy pathways. This is the body system we all think of when we prepare for endurance sports such as swimming, biking, and running. Most new triathletes pay little attention to the muscular system, yet it plays a major role in how well you do in a triathlon. Muscles that are strong and supple make it easier to finish on race day. Weak and tight muscles just don't do very well on hills, in strong winds, in choppy water, and going the distance. Experienced triathletes know this, so they lift weights and stretch regularly to maintain well-balanced muscles.

In the previous three chapters we thoroughly examined swimming, biking, and running. In this chapter we see how triathletes improve their strength and flexibility with weight lifting and stretching.

WHERE DO I FIND THE TIME?

Probably the biggest challenge you will face in getting ready for your first triathlon is time. How are you going to find enough to not only swim, bike, and run but also lift weights and stretch? That's a tall order given how packed your day already is. How can you solve this dilemma?

Let's start with stretching, as it is pretty easy to fit into your day. The best time is the first few minutes right after you swim, bike, or run. But you can also do a little stretching throughout the day at your desk at work, while standing in line at the supermarket, or while watching TV.

Weight lifting, however, is a bit of a challenge for the time-constrained triathlete. The strength exercises at the gym take about forty-five minutes to an hour to complete. But if you haven't got time to go to a gym and you don't have weight equipment at home, there are other options. Most of the exercises in this chapter can be done with elastic resistance bands, which can be purchased at sporting goods stores, through catalogs, and online (www.performbetter.com). In some cases your body weight is enough to facilitate strength improvement. For example, one-leg squats replace leg presses, and push-ups may take the place of bench presses. With a little creativity you can find a way to do most of the gym exercises at home with little or no equipment. Then you can fit strength training into your week more easily. In addition, strength exercises don't have to be done in a single, dedicated workout. You can easily spread them throughout the week, fitting in one or two whenever you have time.

GETTING STRONGER

Is there a downside to lifting weights? Are you afraid of becoming muscle-bound and heavy? Indeed, there are endurance athletes who don't lift weights out of fear that pumping iron may cause an increase in body weight and slow them down. While there are a few younger men who have a tendency to increase muscle mass, it's unlikely with the program I've prepared for you. The strength-building program for triathletes that I use is considerably different than that used by body builders and power lifters. Athletes I coach have never built so much muscle that they gained weight and were slower triathletes; in fact, just the opposite has happened—they have typically become leaner and faster. Building muscle increases the metabolism, which means you burn more calories throughout the day, thus losing excess fat.

Although research reports mixed results, my experience from coaching hundreds of athletes over twenty-five years is that lifting weights definitely improves the performance of those who lack power, and this applies especially to those who are new to triathlon. But it appears to be more effective for some sports than for others. For example, it seems to benefit cycling more than running or swimming, although you will improve some in all three sports.

Not all triathletes or even all cyclists will see noticeable improvement, however. Those most likely to realize a boost in performance, I've found, are women, older men, and athletes with long, lanky arms and legs. Most males in their twenties and early thirties will probably see less improvement than people over fifty.

The biggest factor in determining whether you should lift weights is how much time you have available to do it. If you just can't find a way to fit even a few more minutes of strength-building exercises into your week once you've done your swim, bike, and run workouts, then strength training must be left out. Triathlon-specific training comes before strength training—you never have to lift weights in a triathlon. That's why in the training schedules suggested in Chapter 9 the strength workouts are listed as "optional." Do them if you have time, but otherwise focus on the three sports of triathlon: swimming, biking, and running. However, I suspect that it is possible to do some strength building with a little creative thinking about how you use your time.

STRENGTH-BUILDING ROUTINES

I have set up a strength program for you that doesn't take a lot of time and yet will give you nice results, which basically means your first triathlon will be easier than it might otherwise have been. I've used this program with lots of other triathlon newbies with great success. I think it will work for you also.

You won't be lifting heavy weights, as your muscles will be getting a lot of work already with the other sports, and we don't want to risk injury from overuse. Instead, you will first learn to do the exercises correctly with light weights. After improving your weight-lifting skills we'll make the loads a little heavier to really build strength.

The most important aspect of this program is consistency. Frequently missing strength workouts negates the reason for doing them. If you know now that you can't get into the gym at least once each week, then don't even start. If this is the case, you probably already have more to do in your life than you can fit in and need to devote your available time to swimming, biking, and running. As mentioned earlier, although getting stronger will make you a better triathlete, this is not as important as getting more fit in the three main sports.

In setting up a routine, the first issue is how often and on what days you will go to the gym. The schedule in Chapter 9 suggests two times per week. If you can only go once, that is still effective. You'll still see improvement over time if you're consistent, although not as much as if you worked on strength twice every week. The two days are best separated by 72 to 96 hours. So, for example, one gym session on Monday and another on Thursday or Friday is just right. Putting them closer together than this means there is a big gap in the number of days until the next gym workout the following week. That gap will make the workouts slightly less effective.

The second thing to consider is where you will do the strength-building workouts. I have been referring to the gym, but that may not be an option for you. If you have some strength equipment at home, you can do it there. That may even save you time. Almost every exercise shown below can be done with stretch bands also. These are basically large rubber bands and can be purchased at sporting goods stores, online, or from catalogs.

A lot of triathletes swim at their gym's pool, so they do swim and weight workouts on the same day, one right after the other. This saves time spent driving back and forth. If you do that, make the swim workout the first session each time. It's not a good idea to swim with muscles fatigued from weight lifting; that will cause you to build bad swim habits. If you must do one of the sports right *after* lifting weights, it's best to make that biking, as running on tired legs can easily lead to injury.

HOW MUCH WEIGHT TO USE

Next you need to figure out how much weight to lift. Weight lifters refer to "repetition max," or "RM." What this means is how much weight someone can lift a given number of times. For example, if you can leg press 200 pounds 15 times, your 15RM is 200.

As you start this program to build your strength, you will be lifting 30RM loads, which is quite light. In fact, even though you can lift the load 30 times, you will stop at 20 repetitions the first few times you are in the gym because you want to first become good at doing the exercises. That will take perhaps four strength sessions. After that you will increase the loads to 15RM and do 12 to 15 repetitions. To be on the safe side and to reduce the possibility of lost swim, bike, and run training due to sore muscles, it's best to stop each exercise when you feel like you could only do one or two more reps. Do *not* push to the point of failure—meaning you can't complete even one more rep—on any exercise.

So how do you decide what your 30RM or 15RM is? The only sure way is to test yourself by seeing how many reps you can do with given loads.

Do *not* push to the point of failure—meaning you can't complete even one more rep—on any exercise.

This isn't the best approach for endurance athletes because it always makes them sore for several days afterward. I think you can probably guess your loads pretty well based on what you discover in the first few gym sessions. You don't have to be precise with this, but you do need to challenge yourself a bit every few days. Try increasing the load by 5 percent every third or fourth session to see if you can handle it. If you are progressing normally you should see a steady improvement in strength in the first few weeks.

STRENGTH-BUILDING EXERCISES

One of the most important parts of any strength program is which exercises you will do. There are lots of exercises you could do at the gym to get stronger, but your focus should be only on getting stronger for triathlon. You won't win a body-building contest on this program, but I expect that is okay with you.

It's important that the resistance exercises you do match the movements of the sport for which you are training. For example, there is little reason for a swimmer to do leg presses, but this is a quite valuable exercise for cyclists since the movement comes close to what you do when pedaling a bike. The exercises shown later in this chapter are based on the movements of triathlon and closely mimic them in order to make your triathlon muscles stronger. Also, some of the exercises here may be necessary to help correct muscular imbalances, which may lead to frequent injury.

It's best that the strength exercises involve more than one joint (multi-joint) whenever possible. For example, a seated knee extension is a single-joint exercise because only one joint—the knee—is used (see Figure 8.11). The leg press (see Figure 8.1), however, is a multi-joint exercise involving the hip, knee, and ankle. Multi-joint exercises more closely mimic the movements of triathlon, and they save time in the weight room because larger parts of the body and more muscles can be worked with each exercise. Single-joint exercises are used here to isolate muscles prone to triathlon injury.

The first exercise listed for each muscle group is if you have gym equipment available. If you do not, use the second exercise in each section. These alternative exercises are designed to be done at home with an elastic resistance band or your body weight. There is no reason to do both of the provided exercises.

#1 Leg-Building Exercises

Leg Press (Figure 8.1)

Improves pedaling strength for cycling and hill running power.

1. Center your feet on the middle portion of the platform about 10 to 12 inches apart, center to center. Your feet should be parallel, not angled out, and in the middle of the platform.

2. Press the platform up until your legs are almost straight, with your knees just short of locking out.

3. Lower the platform until your knees are about 8 inches from your chest, no lower. This should create about a 90-degree angle in your knees. (It may help to have a friend check your knee angle to make sure it is about 90 degrees.)

4. Keep your knees in line with your feet throughout the movement— don't let them flare out wide or collapse toward each other.

5. Return to the start position.

FIGURE 8.1 *Leg press*

Elastic Band Squat (Figure 8.2)

Holding the ends of a couple of yards of elastic band, stand with your feet on the middle of the band. Squat until your knees are at a 90-degree bend and then stand back up. Keep your back straight, rear end low, and head up. Stretch the band to increase the tension.

One-Leg Squat (Figure 8.3)

Stand on one leg with the other bent at the knee. Place one hand against a wall to stabilize yourself. Keeping your head up

FIGURE 8.2 *Elastic band squat*

and back straight, bend the support leg to lower yourself until that knee is in a 90-degree angle (have someone help you get this right). Stand back up. Complete all of the repetitions with one leg before doing the other in the same manner.

FIGURE 8.3 *One-leg squat*

#2 Back-Building Exercises

FIGURE 8.4 *Seated row*

Seated Row (Figure 8.4)

Simulates the movement of pulling on the handlebars while climbing a hill on a bicycle in a seated position. Strengthens the core—lower and upper back.

1. Grasp the bar with your arms fully extended and your hands about 10 to 12 inches apart.

2. Pull the bar toward your lower chest, keeping your elbows close to your body.

3. Minimize movement at the waist by using your back muscles to stabilize your position.

4. Return to the start position.

Seated Row with Elastic Band (Figure 8.5)
Sit on the floor with your legs straight out in front of you. While holding each end of the elastic band, loop it under your feet. Bend forward at the waist, keeping your back straight, and stretch the band until it is tight. With a small rowing motion, pull the ends of the band to the sides of your lower chest.

FIGURE 8.5 *Seated row with elastic band*

FIGURE 8.6 *Chest press*

#3 Chest-Building Exercises

Chest Press (Figure 8.6)
Stabilizes the shoulders for swimming and strengthens the shoulder girdle and triceps. Can be done either with free weights or on a machine.

1. Grasp the bars with your hands just slightly farther apart than the width of your shoulders.
2. Slowly lower the bar to your chest.
3. Return to the start position.

FIGURE 8.7 *Push-up*

Push-Up (Figure 8.7)

May be done with either feet or knees as the support points. May also be done on an unstable surface such as a stability ball under your feet or knees or disc pillows under your hands.

I call exercises 4, 5, and 6 "personal weakness" exercises. The idea here is to do only one of these three based on which area of your legs gives you the most trouble, in order to make it stronger. If it is your calves and Achilles (shin splints, sore calves, Achilles tendinitis), then do exercise 4. If your weakness is the muscles and tendons around your knees (cramping or general soreness in the muscles and tendons around your knees), then do exercise 5. And if your weakness is the hamstrings on the back of your upper leg (soreness, tightness, muscle pulls), do exercise 6. If you have more than one such personal weakness area, then do two or all three of these exercises. You may also need to do a lot of stretching for this personal weakness area. That's covered later in this chapter.

#4 Calf-Building Exercises

Heel Raise (Figure 8.8)

If you have experienced calf or Achilles tendon injuries, this exercise may help to strengthen those tissues. It also improves lower leg strength for running.

1. Stand with the balls of your feet on a 1- to 2-inch rider such as a board, with your heels on the floor and a barbell on your shoulders or a dumbbell in each hand.

2. Your feet should be pointed straight ahead and about shoulder width apart.
3. Raise up on your toes.
4. Return to the start position.

Elastic Band Toe Raises (Figure 8.9)

Assume the same position as in steps 1 and 2 above, only with an elastic band under the balls of your feet and the ends of it in each hand, with your arms straight down at your sides. Complete the movement as in steps 3 and 4. Shorten the elastic band to increase the load.

FIGURE 8.8 *Heel raise*

FIGURE 8.9 *Elastic band toe raises*

FIGURE 8.10 *Knee extension*

#5 Knee-Strengthening Exercises

Knee Extension (Figure 8.10)

If you have had knee problems in the past, this exercise may help by balancing the strength between your medial and lateral quadriceps. It's a good idea to check with your doctor if you have had knee problems to make sure this is the correct exercise for your unique knee history.

1. Start with your knees fully extended and toes pointing slightly to the outside, as in Figure 8.10.

2. Lower the weight only about 8 inches (do *not* go all the way down—you may be able to lock the machine out to prevent your foot from going too low).

3. Return to the starting position.

Knee Extension with Elastic Band (Figure 8.11)

This one is difficult to simulate at home, but here is one alternative. You may be able to come up with a better one. Sit in a straight-backed chair with your legs crossed so that your left knee is resting on your right leg. Loop an elastic band over your left ankle and under your right foot. Straighten

FIGURE 8.11 *Knee extension with elastic band*

your left knee, raising your lower leg to the horizontal position. Lower it and repeat. Shorten the elastic band to increase the tension.

#6 Hamstring-Building Exercises

Leg Curl (Figure 8.12)

By strengthening the hamstrings on the back of the upper leg, the balance of strength between that muscle and the larger quadriceps on the front of the thigh is improved. This may help to prevent hamstring injuries in athletes who are plagued by this problem. Leg curl machines are used either standing (shown here), seated, or on the stomach.

Pull your knee toward your rear end until your knee is at about a 90-degree angle (have someone help you get this right). Don't allow your rear end to arch upward.

Return to the start position.

FIGURE 8.12 *Leg curl*

Assisted Leg Curl (Figure 8.13)

You'll need a helper for this one. Lay on your stomach on the floor with your helper at your feet. The helper holds onto the heel of one foot as you pull it toward your rear end. The helper should provide just enough resistance to make the foot move up slowly. Return to the start position and repeat.

FIGURE 8.13 *Assisted leg curl*

#7 Abdominal-Building Exercises

Abdominal with Twist (Figure 8.14)

This is a basic core exercise to help stabilize your body while swimming, biking, and running.

1. Sit on a decline board with your knees bent at about a 90-degree angle.
2. Cross your arms over your chest. Holding a weight plate against your chest is optional. (Do *not* pull on your head or neck.)

FIGURE 8.14 *Abdominal with twist*

3. Lower your body to about a 45-degree angle to the floor.
4. Return to the start position with a twist of your upper body. With each repetition, alternate twisting to the right and left as you raise up.

Crunches with Twist (Figure 8.15)

Assume the same position as in Figure 8.14 only on the floor. When you curl up, alternate touching your right elbow to your left leg and your left elbow to your right leg.

FIGURE 8.15 *Crunches with twist*

#8 Shoulder-Building Exercises

Standing, Bent-Arm Lat Pull Down (Figure 8.16)

This increases the strength of your shoulders to make swimming easier.

1. While standing (or on your knees) at the lat pull-down station, position the bar so it is a few inches above your head.

2. Place your hands on top of the bar about shoulder width apart, with your elbows slightly bent.

3. Maintain a high elbow position and push the bar down by rotating your shoulder until the bar is at chest level.

4. Return to the start position.

Elastic Band Lat Pull (Figure 8.17)

Open a door and stand facing the edge of it so that you can have one arm on either side. Place your elastic band over the top of the door so that it hangs down on both sides. Grasp both ends of the band and pull down, following the instructions above.

FIGURE 8.16 *Standing, bent-arm lat pull down*

STRENGTH PHASES

In the next chapter you will learn about *periodization,* which organizes your training to improve fitness. Basically, this is a way of systematically scheduling variety into your training program so that you are race-

FIGURE 8.17 *Elastic band lat pull*

ready when you get to your first triathlon. Your strength training is a part of this scheduling process, so you will vary the workouts a bit every few weeks. This variety is based on different periods, or "phases," of strength training, each of which has a specific purpose.

You will use three phases of training in your strength routine over the twelve weeks as you prepare for your first triathlon: *anatomical adaptation* (AA), *maximum transition* (MT), and *strength maintenance* (SM). Each lasts a few weeks, just enough time to accomplish its purpose. Table 8.1 brings together everything about your strength training in one place. This same pattern is built into your twelve-week training plan in Chapter 9.

Here are the three phases of your strength-training program.

Anatomical Adaptation

The purpose of anatomical adaptation is to prepare the muscles and tendons for the heavier work of the MT phase and to perfect the movements of each exercise. More exercises are done in this phase than in the other two because improved general body strength is a goal. In AA you do three sets of each exercise. A "set" is a number of repetitions of an exercise. In AA the first twenty reps are done to completion, then you stop to rest. That's the first set finished, and you have

TABLE 8.1	STRENGTH TRAINING AT A GLANCE					
Phase	Weeks to Tri	Workouts/ Week	Exercises	Load	Sets	Reps
AA	12	2	1, 2, 3 (4, 5, or 6), 7, 8	30RM	3	20
AA	11	2	1, 2, 3 (4, 5, or 6), 7, 8	30RM	3	20
MT	10	2	1, 2 (4, 5, or 6), 7, 8	20RM	3	15–20
MT	9	2	1, 2 (4, 5, or 6), 7, 8	15RM	3	10–15
MT	8	2	1, 2 (4, 5, or 6), 7, 8	15RM	3	10–15
MT	7	2	1, 2 (4, 5, or 6), 7, 8	15RM	3	10–15
SM	6	1	1, 2 (4, 5, or 6), 7, 8	20, 15RM	2	10–15
SM	5	1	1, 2 (4, 5, or 6), 7, 8	20, 15RM	2	10–15
SM	4	1	1, 2 (4, 5, or 6), 7, 8	20, 15RM	2	10–15
SM	3	1	1, 2 (4, 5, or 6), 7, 8	20, 15RM	2	10–15
SM	2	1	1, 2 (4, 5, or 6), 7, 8	20, 15RM	2	10–15
--	1	0	--	--	--	--

two more to go. After the next two sets are completed, you move on to the next exercise and complete three sets of it. The loads are very light (30RM), easily allowing for a high number of reps (twenty). You could do more than twenty reps, but don't, because what you want to accomplish with this workout is perfection of technique, and doing more will cause fatigue, resulting in sloppy technique. After four of these workouts in two weeks you will begin to notice that you are already getting stronger.

Maximum Transition

This is really the heart of your strength-building program for this twelve-week period. If you felt like you were getting stronger in AA, you'll notice an even bigger change after eight of these workouts. The number of exercises are pared back a bit so you can focus on getting stronger in the most triathlon-specific areas (these are listed for each week in the training plan in Chapter 9). The loads increase the first week to 20RM, and you do fifteen to twenty reps. These two sessions are a transition period, allowing you to adjust to heavier loads and make sure you are getting the weight right. During the next three weeks the loads are increased to 15RM, and you do ten to fifteen reps. Stop each set when you feel that you can only do one or two more reps. The number of reps you can complete on a given day may vary depending on how tired you are from your swim, bike, and run workouts. Don't let that bother you; it's normal.

Strength Maintenance

The purpose of SM is to maintain the strength you've built in the previous weeks of the MT phase. It takes only about half as much work to maintain a given level of fitness as it took to achieve it. That means you can maintain your strength once you have thoroughly developed it by only lifting weights once per week instead of twice. It also means that you only have to do one heavy set of each exercise to stay strong.

In SM, when you do strength exercises one day a week you will do one light set (20RM) to warm up, followed by one heavy set (15RM) to maintain strength. For both sets you will do ten to fifteen reps. This means the warm-up set will be quite easy and the heavy set quite hard. This will keep you strong for the next several weeks.

You don't need to memorize Table 8.1 and these explanations because this routine is built into your training plan in Chapter 9. They are included here so you can see the details of what you will be doing in the coming weeks.

BECOMING MORE FLEXIBLE

Some people are just naturally flexible. While standing they can put their palms on the floor easily, touch their fingers behind their shoulder blades, squat without falling over backward, and sit on the floor with their legs spread apart, touching their noses to their knees. Most of us aren't so flexibly endowed. If you're naturally tight you need to become more flexible. If you are already "loose as a goose" in all of your joints then you need not spend much time stretching. It's rare to find such total-body flexibility, however. Someone who has flexible shoulders may well be tight in the hips. My experience has been that practically every triathlete benefits from stretching several times a week.

> Most of us aren't so flexibly endowed. If you're naturally tight you need to become more flexible. If you are already "loose as a goose" in all of your joints then you need not spend much time stretching.

Of the three sports, swimming requires the most flexibility, especially in the shoulders and ankles. If your shoulders are tight, you'll have a hard time getting your elbow above your hand on the recovery part of the stroke, creating an inefficient, zigzag swim technique. People with tight ankles who are new to swimming often go backward when they use a kickboard. If your hamstrings are tight, you are prone to biking and running injuries. Tight, inflexible hamstrings also contribute to low back problems, which is at epidemic proportions in North America. Biking will tend to make your quads (thighs) tight, and running contributes to tight calf muscles and thus shin pain for newbies.

If you are tight in any of these areas, a little time spent stretching every day may well prevent soreness and injury and make you a better triathlete. Prevention is always more comfortable, less time-consuming, and cheaper than medical treatment.

HOW TO STRETCH

There are as many different ways to stretch as there are types of bicycles. And just as with bikes, each kind of stretching has unique advantages and disadvantages. This creates a lot of confusion. You will use the easiest and most common form of stretching—*static stretching*.

Static stretching has been around since the 1970s and is still the most widely used method of triathletes. It's really quite simple. Take a position that stretches a given muscle group and hold it for several seconds. You may find that some tight muscles feel best when stretched this way for fifteen to twenty seconds. For others eight to twelve seconds feels right. The key to static stretching is not so much how long you hold the position, but how frequently you stretch.

A few seconds spent stretching different muscles throughout the day will greatly improve your flexibility over time. Good times to stretch are before and after workouts and at the end of your day just before bed. Each of these may take only five minutes or so. It's also easy to fit little stretches, such as shin stretching by pointing your toes, into your day when at your desk, standing in line at the checkout, or riding in a car.

STRETCHING EXERCISES

Although stretching does not have to be a specific routine, there are a few stretches that will directly aid your swimming, biking, and running. Following are a few that work well before and after workouts. You may also want to use others that you've found to be beneficial.

Shoulder Reach (Figure 8.18)

This is a great exercise to do before and after swimming to improve the flexibility of your shoulders.

1. Extend your arms over your head and cross one wrist over the other while interlocking your hands.
2. With your elbows behind your ears, straighten your arms and reach up.

FIGURE 8.18 *Shoulder reach*

Ankle Sit (Figure 8.19)

Another swimming exercise, this sit will loosen tight ankles, allowing you to be more streamlined in the water.

1. Sit on your shins on a padded surface or folded towel with your toes pointed (not splayed to the sides).
2. Sit on your heels.
3. Lean backward slightly until you feel an easy stretch.

FIGURE 8.19 *Ankle sit*

Twister (Figure 8.20)

This exercise will help you become more flexible in the shoulders, allowing your arm recovery movement in swimming to be much easier.

1. With your back facing a wall, grasp a stationary object at about shoulder height.

2. Look away from the arm being stretched and twist your body away from it also.

Stork Stand (Figure 8.21)

This exercise works well for both biking and running but is especially beneficial before and after a bike ride.

FIGURE 8.20 *Twister*

1. While balancing against your bike or a wall, grasp your *right* foot behind your back with your *left* hand.
2. Gently pull up and *away* from your rear end with your hand.
3. Keep your head up and stand tall—do *not* bend over at the waist.

Triangle (Figure 8.22)

Stretching the hamstrings this way is beneficial to both running and biking.

FIGURE 8.21 *Stork stand*

1. Bend over at the waist while leaning on your bike or a wall.
2. Place the leg to be stretched forward, with your foot about 18 inches from the bike or wall.
3. Keep the other leg directly behind the first. The farther back this leg is placed, the greater the stretch.
4. With your weight on the front foot, sag your upper body toward the floor. You should feel the stretch in the hamstring (back of the thigh) of your forward leg.

FIGURE 8.22 *Triangle*

Pull Down (Figure 8.23)

This is especially good for shoulder flexibility for swimming but also relieves tightness due to biking and running.

1. Hold on to your bike or a railing for balance, with your weight resting on your arms.

2. Allow your head to sag deeply between your outstretched arms to create a stretch in your lats (sides of the torso).

FIGURE 8.23 *Pull down*

FIGURE 8.24 *Squat*

Squat (Figure 8.24)

The squat is a great lower back and leg stretch for running and biking. If you don't have time for any others, this is the one to do.

1. Holding on to something for balance, squat down, keeping your heels on the floor (this is easier with your bike shoes off).

2. Allow your rear end to sag close to your heels as you rock forward.

Wall Lean (Figure 8.25)

This is probably the most popular running stretch of all time. It helps to loosen up tight calf muscles.

1. Lean against a wall, with the leg to be stretched straight behind you and the other forward, holding most of your weight.

FIGURE 8.25 *Wall lean*

2. Keep the heel of the rear foot on the floor, with the toes pointed straight ahead.

3. The farther forward your hips move, the greater the stretch on your calf.

4. There are two major calf muscles. To stretch the other one, bend your rear knee.

Chapter 9

YOUR TRAINING PLAN

Are you feeling overwhelmed yet? There is so much to learn about the sport of triathlon that it can leave you a bit snowed under. But don't worry; everyone goes through this.

Training in one sport, such as running, is hard enough. Training in three sports at the same time is more than three times as challenging in part because you need to blend so many different workouts into a week. When preparing for a triathlon you obviously can't do as much swimming as a swimmer does. The same goes for biking and running. Athletes in each of these sports put in far more training time and distance in their sports than does the typical triathlete. For example, the average beginner athlete in each of these sports probably exercises around five to six hours each week. If you tried to do what each of them do, you'd have to exercise fifteen to eighteen hours a week, and that does not include strength training. Obviously that is not going to happen.

Assuming you have around three to four hours each week to work out, you need to figure out how to make the best use of that time so your fitness improves steadily. If you overdo it you may easily become overtrained, injured, or sick. But if you do too little your fitness won't improve enough to finish your first triathlon. This is the quandary every new triathlete faces.

The purpose of this chapter is to help you solve that problem by providing a training plan you can follow and modify as necessary. It's not possible to have a one-schedule-fits-all training plan; there are just too many variables, such as time available to exercise, prior experience in one or more sports, how quickly one recovers, and individual rates of fitness improvement. So I've designed this training plan with optional workouts based on your unique situation.

Why should you even have a plan? Why not just swim, bike, run, and do strength workouts when you have the time? That may work for a few people, but chances are it won't work for you. I expect you are like most triathletes—very busy, with too much to do already. And yet somehow you are going to try to wedge triathlon training into each day. If you don't have a plan of what you will do every day, chances are you won't do much. A well-defined plan keeps you on schedule to achieve your goal. I have made your plan as user-friendly and flexible as possible so you can stay on track.

Before we get down to the nuts and bolts of a training plan, let's review a few basic concepts on how to get fit.

THE BIG PICTURE: HOW TO GET FIT

The plan I've put together for you in this chapter is based on a system of training called *periodization*. As mentioned in Chapter 8, this is really nothing more than a way of organizing training so that you train hard when you need to, rest when you need to, and are race-fit the day of your race. Using periodization, your weekly hours of training will increase steadily as you get in better condition and are able to handle more. Essentially, your workouts will become progressively longer.

They will also become more like the triathlon for which you are training by requiring more effort. If there are going to be hills on the triathlon course, eventually you will have to include hills in your workouts. If your first triathlon will be in what is usually a hot time of year, you will need to practice in the heat as you get closer to race day. All of this is called *training specificity*—your workouts will become increasingly more like the race over time.

The most important aspect of preparation for your first triathlon is *consistency*. There's no doubt that you will miss some workouts, but you can't miss many.

Occasionally there will be days when something pops up in your life and prevents you from getting on your bike right after work as you had planned, such as the boss asking you to work overtime. There will be some Saturday when taking the kids out of town to a soccer game will be more important. You may also catch a flu bug and miss a few days of training. It's important to keep such interruptions to your training plan to a minimum. If missing workouts becomes a weekly occurrence, your chances of achieving your triathlon goal will be greatly diminished.

Experienced triathletes have developed coping strategies for these interruptions to training. Seasoned triathletes will take a bike and a stationary trainer to the soccer match and ride while watching the game. They will run during their lunch break on days they need to work late. They get up earlier to work out on mornings when they have to be at an early meeting. They watch the big game on TV while riding a stationary bike rather than missing either the game or the ride. To get in shape for your first triathlon, you will have to become a master at such coping strategies. If you allow life to get in the way of your workouts too often, you just won't be ready.

YOUR TRAINING PLAN

Four plans are offered here to help you organize your training. You don't have to use them if you already have a good idea of how to prepare yourself for your first triathlon. These plans allow twelve weeks for you to get in shape. If you're starting from ground zero, that should be just about right. If you have been working out for a few weeks you can jump in at a level that closely matches what you are doing now.

The beginner plan (Table 9.1) is for the person who is brand new to all three sports. It will help you gradually build fitness in swimming, biking, and running. The swimmer plan (Table 9.2) is intended for the person who has a good background in that sport and usually works out with a masters swim group. If you're an accomplished swimmer who trains alone, then simply plug in your own swim workouts on the days calling for a masters swim. The cyclist plan (Table 9.3) offers much harder and longer bike workouts for the experienced and fit bike rider. If this describes you, I have a suggestion. Many serious cyclists do most of their riding with groups in mini-races. You should avoid these when training for a triathlon because the recovery "cost" is just too high and will cut into your swim and run training. The runner plan (Table 9.4) is for the person who has a running background and has built up considerable fitness in this sport. The running workouts here are much more challenging than in the other three plans. Common features of the plans are described below.

Workouts

The plans refer to workouts by number, such as "Bike #2." Each workout description can be found in the appropriate appendix. The swim workouts are in Appendix B, the bike workouts in Appendix C, run workouts in Appendix D, combination workouts in Appendix E, and strength workouts in Appendix F.

Intensities

Each of the workouts in the appendixes tells you how hard to exercise, using this "Rating of Perceived Exertion" (RPE) scale:

Zone 1	Very easy with light breathing
Zone 2	Easy with increased breathing
Zone 3	Moderately hard with somewhat labored breathing
Zone 4	Hard with labored breathing
Zone 5	Very hard with panting

This scale may be used for all sports but is the only one used for swimming workouts. For the bike and run workouts, if you are using a heart rate monitor, refer to your heart rate training zones, which you can calculate using the method shown on pages 149–150 in Chapter 10. You don't have to use a heart rate monitor; RPE is fine.

Optional Workouts

Most weeks in the plans have two swim, two bike, and two run workouts scheduled. Beginning at six weeks to go until your first triathlon, combination (bike + run) workouts are included. There are also optional swim, bike, run, and strength workouts included for each week. These are workouts you may do if you have the time, but they aren't necessary if you just want to finish the triathlon. The experienced swimmer, cyclist, or runner may want to do the optional workout in his or her sport to maintain a higher level of fitness.

Combination Workouts

These training sessions, combining biking and running into one workout, are the key to doing well in triathlon. Over the course of several weeks they become mini-triathlons and get you ready for the challenge of completing two or more sports without rest.

Recovery and Rejuvenation Weeks

Recovery and rejuvenation weeks are built into the plans at nine, six, and three weeks before your first triathlon. During these weeks consider cutting back even more if you are especially tired or feeling pressured to keep up with everything in your life. It is perfectly fine to not do the optional workouts or to leave out one or more of the primary workouts in order to rest more. These mini-breaks will allow you to physically rest and mentally rejuvenate. There will be no loss of fitness. In fact, after resting more than usual you will probably feel like you gained fitness.

Race Week

The last two weeks on each schedule are called "1 Week to Tri on Saturday" and "1 Week to Tri on Sunday." Follow only one of these weekly plans, depending on which day your first triathlon is to be held.

| TABLE 9.1 | BEGINNER PLAN |

	Monday	**Tuesday**	**Wednesday**
12 Weeks to Tri	Optional strength #1 or day off	Swim #1 and optional run #1	Bike #1
11 Weeks to Tri	Optional strength #1 or day off	Swim #1 and optional run #1	Bike #2
10 Weeks to Tri	Optional strength #2 or day off	Swim #2 and optional run #2	Bike #1
9 Weeks to Tri (R&R)	Optional strength #3 or day off	Swim #2 and optional run #3	Bike #5
8 Weeks to Tri	Optional strength #3 or day off	Swim #3 and optional run #8	Bike #1
7 Weeks to Tri	Optional strength #3 or day off	Swim #3 and optional run #4	Bike #7
6 Weeks to Tri (R&R)	Optional strength #4 or day off	Swim #4 and optional run #8	Bike #7
5 Weeks to Tri	Optional strength #4 or day off	Swim #4 and optional run #4	Bike #9
4 Weeks to Tri	Optional strength #4 or day off	Swim #5 and optional run #8	Bike #8
3 Weeks to Tri (R&R)	Optional strength #4 or day off	Swim #5 and optional run #8	Bike #8
2 Weeks to Tri	Optional strength #4 or day off	Swim #5 and optional run #4	Bike #9
1 Week to Tri on Saturday	Day off	Bike #3	Run #1
1 Week to Tri on Sunday	Day off	Swim #5	Bike #3

Note: Workout details are in Appendixes B (swim), C (bike), D (run), E (combination), and F (strength).

Thursday	Friday	Saturday	Sunday
Run #8 and optional strength #1	Swim #1 and optional bike #1	Bike #2	Run #1 and optional swim #1
Run #8 and optional strength #1	Swim #1 and optional bike #1	Bike #3	Run #2 and optional swim #1
Run #8 and optional strength #2	Swim #2 and optional bike #3	Bike #4	Run #3 and optional swim #1
Run #8 and optional strength #3	Swim #2 and optional bike #3	Bike #9	Run #4 and optional swim #1
Run #3 and optional strength #3	Swim #3 and optional bike #1	Bike #9	Run #4 and optional swim #1
Run #8 and optional strength #3	Swim #3 and optional bike #3	Bike #10	Run #5 and optional swim #1
Run #4	Swim #4 and optional bike #3	Run #5	Optional swim #1 and combination #1
Run #8	Swim #4 and optional bike #2	Run #6	Optional swim #1 and combination #2
Run #6	Swim #6 and optional bike #3	Bike #9 and optional swim #1	Swim #6 and combination #3
Run #7	Swim #6 and optional bike #3	Bike #3 and optional swim #1	Swim #6 and combination #4
Run #8	Swim #6 and optional bike #1	Bike #1 and optional swim #1	Swim #6 and combination #3
Swim #2	Bike #1	**Your First Triathlon**	Day off
Run #1	Swim #2	Bike #1	**Your First Triathlon**

| TABLE 9.2 | SWIMMER PLAN |

	Monday	**Tuesday**	**Wednesday**
12 Weeks to Tri	Optional strength #1 or day off	Swim #7 and optional run #1	Bike #1
11 Weeks to Tri	Optional strength #1 or day off	Swim #7 and optional run #1	Bike #2
10 Weeks to Tri	Optional strength #2 or day off	Swim #7 and optional run #2	Bike #1
9 Weeks to Tri (R&R)	Optional strength #3 or day off	Swim #7 and optional run #3	Bike #5
8 Weeks to Tri	Optional strength #3 or day off	Swim #7 and optional run #8	Bike #1
7 Weeks to Tri	Optional strength #3 or day off	Swim #7 and optional run #4	Bike #7
6 Weeks to Tri (R&R)	Optional strength #4 or day off	Swim #7 and optional run #8	Bike #7
5 Weeks to Tri	Optional strength #4 or day off	Swim #7 and optional run #4	Bike #9
4 Weeks to Tri	Optional strength #4 or day off	Swim #7 and optional run #8	Bike #8
3 Weeks to Tri (R&R)	Optional strength #4 or day off	Swim #7 and optional run #8	Bike #8
2 Weeks to Tri	Optional strength #4 or day off	Swim #7 and optional run #4	Bike #9
1 Week to Tri on Saturday	Day off	Bike #3	Run #1
1 Week to Tri on Sunday	Day off	Swim #5	Bike #3

Note: Workout details are in Appendixes B (swim), C (bike), D (run), E (combination), and F (strength).

Thursday	Friday	Saturday	Sunday
Run #8 and optional strength #1	Swim #7 and optional bike #1	Bike #2	Run #1 and optional swim #8
Run #8 and optional strength #1	Swim #7 and optional bike #1	Bike #3	Run #2 and optional swim #8
Run #8 and optional strength #2	Swim #7 and optional bike #3	Bike #4	Run #3 and optional swim #8
Run #8 and optional strength #3	Swim #7 and optional bike #3	Bike #9	Run #4 and optional swim #8
Run #3 and optional strength #3	Swim #7 and optional bike #1	Bike #9	Run #4 and optional swim #8
Run #8 and optional strength #3	Swim #7 and optional bike #3	Bike #10	Run #5 and optional swim #8
Run #4	Swim #7 and optional bike #3	Run #5	Optional swim #8 and combination #1
Run #8	Swim #7 and optional bike #2	Run #6	Optional swim #8 and combination #2
Run #6	Swim #7 and optional bike #3	Bike #9 and optional swim #8	Swim #6 and combination #3
Run #7	Swim #7 and optional bike #3	Bike #3 and optional swim #8	Swim #6 and combination #4
Run #8	Swim #7 and optional bike #1	Bike #1 and optional swim #8	Swim #6 and combination #3
Swim #2	Bike #1	**Your First Triathlon**	Day off
Run #1	Swim #4	Bike #1	**Your First Triathlon**

TABLE 9.3 | **CYCLIST PLAN**

	Monday	Tuesday	Wednesday
12 Weeks to Tri	Optional strength #1 or day off	Swim #1 and optional run #1	Bike #8
11 Weeks to Tri	Optional strength #1 or day off	Swim #1 and optional run #1	Bike #8
10 Weeks to Tri	Optional strength #2 or day off	Swim #2 and optional run #2	Bike #8
9 Weeks to Tri (R&R)	Optional strength #3 or day off	Swim #2 and optional run #3	Bike #8
8 Weeks to Tri	Optional strength #3 or day off	Swim #3 and optional run #8	Bike #10
7 Weeks to Tri	Optional strength #3 or day off	Swim #3 and optional run #4	Bike #15
6 Weeks to Tri (R&R)	Optional strength #4 or day off	Swim #4 and optional run #8	Bike #15
5 Weeks to Tri	Optional strength #4 or day off	Swim #4 and optional run #4	Bike #10
4 Weeks to Tri	Optional strength #4 or day off	Swim #5 and optional run #8	Bike #15
3 Weeks to Tri (R&R)	Optional strength #4 or day off	Swim #5 and optional run #8	Bike #15
2 Weeks to Tri	Optional strength #4 or day off	Swim #5 and optional run #4	Bike #10
1 Week to Tri on Saturday	Day off	Bike #4	Run #1
1 Week to Tri on Sunday	Day off	Swim #5	Bike #4

Note: Workout details are in Appendixes B (swim), C (bike), D (run), E (combination), and F (strength).

Thursday	Friday	Saturday	Sunday
Run #8 and optional strength #1	Swim #1 and optional bike #10	Bike #14	Run #1 and optional swim #1
Run #8 and optional strength #1	Swim #1 and optional bike #10	Bike #14	Run #2 and optional swim #1
Run #8 and optional strength #2	Swim #2 and optional bike #10	Bike #14	Run #3 and optional swim #1
Run #8 and optional strength #3	Swim #2 and optional bike #10	Bike #14	Run #4 and optional swim #1
Run #3 and optional strength #3	Swim #3 and optional bike #10	Bike #13	Run #4 and optional swim #1
Run #8 and optional strength #3	Swim #3 and optional bike #10	Bike #14	Run #5 and optional swim #1
Run #4	Swim #4 and optional bike #10	Run #5 and optional bike #13	Optional swim #1 and combination #1
Run #8	Swim #4 and optional bike #10	Run #6 and optional bike #10	Optional swim #1 and combination #2
Run #6	Swim #6 and optional bike #10	Bike #13 and optional swim #1	Swim #6 and combination #3
Run #7	Swim #6 and optional bike #10	Bike #13 and optional swim #1	Swim #6 and combination #4
Run #8	Swim #6 and optional bike #10	Bike #10 and optional swim #1	Swim #6 and combination #3
Swim #2	Bike #1	**Your First Triathlon**	Day off
Run #1	Swim #2	Bike #1	**Your First Triathlon**

	Monday	**Tuesday**	**Wednesday**
12 Weeks to Tri	Optional strength #1 or day off	Swim #1 and optional run #9	Bike #1
11 Weeks to Tri	Optional strength #1 or day off	Swim #1 and optional run #9	Bike #2
10 Weeks to Tri	Optional strength #2 or day off	Swim #2 and optional run #9	Bike #1
9 Weeks to Tri (R&R)	Optional strength #3 or day off	Swim #2 and optional run #9	Bike #5
8 Weeks to Tri	Optional strength #3 or day off	Swim #3 and optional run #8	Bike #1
7 Weeks to Tri	Optional strength #3 or day off	Swim #3 and optional run #9	Bike #7
6 Weeks to Tri (R&R)	Optional strength #4 or day off	Swim #4 and optional run #8	Bike #7
5 Weeks to Tri	Optional strength #4 or day off	Swim #4 and optional run #9	Bike #9
4 Weeks to Tri	Optional strength #4 or day off	Swim #5 and optional run #8	Bike #8
3 Weeks to Tri (R&R)	Optional strength #4 or day off	Swim #5 and optional run #8	Bike #8
2 Weeks to Tri	Optional strength #4 or day off	Swim #5 and optional run #9	Bike #9
1 Week to Tri on Saturday	Day off	Bike #3	Run #8
1 Week to Tri on Sunday	Day off	Swim #5	Bike #3

TABLE 9.4 | **RUNNER PLAN**

Note: Workout details are in Appendixes B (swim), C (bike), D (run), E (combination), and F (strength).

Thursday	Friday	Saturday	Sunday
Run #8 and optional strength #1	Swim #1 and optional bike #1	Bike #2	Run #12 and optional swim #1
Run #8 and optional strength #1	Swim #1 and optional bike #1	Bike #3	Run #12 and optional swim #1
Run #8 and optional strength #2	Swim #2 and optional bike #3	Bike #4	Run #12 and optional swim #1
Run #8 and optional strength #3	Swim #2 and optional bike #3	Bike #9	Run #12 and optional swim #1
Run #9 and optional strength #3	Swim #3 and optional bike #1	Bike #9	Run #10 and optional swim #1
Run #11 and optional strength #3	Swim #3 and optional bike #3	Bike #10	Run #10 and optional swim #1
Run #11	Swim #4 and optional bike #3	Run #10	Optional swim #1 and combination #1
Run #11	Swim #4 and optional bike #2	Run #10	Optional swim #1 and combination #2
Run #11	Swim #6 and optional bike #3	Bike #9 and optional swim #1	Swim #6 and combination #3
Run #11	Swim #6 and optional bike #3	Bike #3 and optional swim #1	Swim #6 and combination #4
Run #8	Swim #6 and optional bike #1	Bike #1 and optional swim #1	Swim #6 and combination #3
Swim #2	Bike #1	**Your First Triathlon**	Day off
Run #8	Swim #2	Bike #1	**Your First Triathlon**

▶ SHOULD YOU EXERCISE WITH A COLD?

Training hard makes you a candidate for an upper respiratory infection. As the workload increases, so does the risk of catching a cold or the flu.

A few years ago a study of entrants in the Los Angeles Marathon found that those who ran more than 60 miles per week had twice as many illnesses as those running less than 20. Also, runners who completed the marathon were six times as likely to be ill the week following the race as those who registered but did not show up to run it.

What you do in the 6 hours following a hard workout or race is critical to your health. During this brief window of time, the immune system is depressed and less capable of fighting off disease. This is a good time to avoid people and public places. Wash your hands after having contact with others or with public facilities. Try to develop the habit of touching your face only with your non-dominant hand and touching objects, such as doors and telephones, with your dominant hand. Take extra care of yourself for these six hours.

What should you do when even after taking all of these precautions you feel a cold coming on—continue training as normal, reduce training, or rest? A "neck check" will help you decide. If you have above-the-neck symptoms, such as a runny nose or a scratchy throat, start your workout, but reduce the intensity and duration. You may begin to feel better once you're warmed up, but if not, stop. If the symptoms are below the neck—such as a sore throat, chest cold, chills, coughing up matter, achy muscles, or a fever—don't even start. These are often symptoms of a virus. Exercising will make it worse.

Even after a flu bug departs, you're likely to experience a decrease in performance for some time. How long depends on the type and severity of the illness. One study found a 15 percent reduction in muscle strength that lasted up to a month following a virus. It may take three months to return to your previous level of aero-

> ### Should You Exercise with a Cold?
>
> bic capacity after an especially bad case of the flu. During this time muscles may produce more lactic acid at lower levels of intensity than before the illness. You may also feel weak for some time.
>
> Training with the flu will not bring improved fitness. Complete rest is needed. Let your body's energy reserves go into fighting the bug rather than trying to recover from workouts. ⊛

WHAT TO DO WHEN THINGS DON'T GO RIGHT

As I discussed above, you're going to miss some workouts. There will be days when life gets in the way of exercise. You'll have to go to work late or early, the kids will need a chauffeur, there will be no pool on a business trip or vacation, unexpected house guests will arrive, or something else will prevent you from doing a workout. An occasional missed workout will have no negative consequences for your first triathlon, but I must stress that repeatedly missing workouts, such as once or twice a week, will considerably reduce your fitness.

Although you can usually forget about the missed workout and continue on with your training plan as if nothing has happened, combination workouts should not be missed because they are very important to your preparation. If you can anticipate that you will miss one of these workouts, try rearranging your workouts for that week so that you can fit it in and leave out another one in the sport at which you are strongest. If you do the optional strength workouts, they should always be the first to cut.

Chapter 10

YOUR HIGH-TECH GEAR

Chapters 5, 6, and 7 described the basic swim, bike, and run equipment you need for your first triathlon. This chapter takes a look at the high-tech gear that is also used by many triathletes. Be forewarned: The equipment described here is *really* high-tech and takes a considerable amount of dedicated use to master. While these devices can help in some small way to make you a better athlete, they are still nothing but tools. You don't *need* to use any of this stuff. Even though they have the potential to make your training more precise and offer a slight boost to your fitness, it's questionable whether a newcomer to the sport needs such precision. Your fitness will improve dramatically without any advanced technology.

There are some people, however, who simply like technology. I'm one of them. I've always enjoyed tinkering with gadgets that could measure and help me analyze what my body is experiencing when swimming, biking, and running. So if you're into technology, this chapter is for you. If not, skip this chapter and continue to keep training simple. Later on, once you are thoroughly hooked on triathlon, you may start looking for ways to get a slight edge in fitness. That's when you'll come back to this chapter, because the equipment described here can make a difference.

There is more technology available for triathlon than for any other endurance sport. You can monitor heart rate, training zones, bicycle power, pace, time, elevation, grade changes, and more if you have all the gear described here. Many triathletes do, and they spend nearly as much time analyzing data after workouts as they spend in training. Some have elaborate records of such training metrics going back years. A few have even created complex spreadsheets that allow them to easily enter and retrieve data. If you would like to collect such personal data but don't want the bother of building spreadsheets, go to www.TrainingPeaks.com, where easy upload and analysis functions are available for a small monthly subscription fee. You'll also find lots of other features there to improve your training.

There are currently three high-tech gadgets available for swimming, biking, and running—heart rate monitors, bicycle power meters, and GPS devices. Before buying any of these, learn more about them and then do some shopping for the best deals. Following is a short discussion of these three pieces of equipment. Remember, they are not necessary, and by themselves they will not make you a better triathlete. As a matter of fact, most pro triathletes do not use high-tech stuff, preferring instead to simply swim, bike, and run based on how they feel.

HEART RATE MONITORS

In training for your first triathlon, there are only four things you can change to improve fitness.

Mode

This is the type of exercise you do—swim, bike, or run. Of course, strength and stretching exercises are also modes of exercise.

Frequency

This if how often you train. If you exercise once each day, your frequency is seven per week.

Duration

This is how long your workouts are, either in time or distance. Combining duration (how long) with frequency (how often) gives you "volume"—how much total training you do for a given period of time, such as a week. When a triathlete says she trained six hours this week, she is talking about both duration and frequency.

Intensity

This is how hard or easy your exercise is. The first three aspects are easy to measure and talk about. Intensity is a little more challenging. For example, when asked how hard you ran today you might say, "It was easy." This really doesn't tell the other person exactly what you did. So you could say, "On a scale of 1 to 5, with 5 being hardest, it was a 2." That's more descriptive. You could also say, "I ran a 10-minute per mile pace on average." That's even more precise. Or you could say, "My heart rate was around 130 beats per minute all the way." Of course, even though heart rate is a good way to express (and control) intensity, it's not very practical to keep stopping to check your heart rate. You can resolve this problem by purchasing a heart rate monitor.

In 1978 a Finnish company, Polar Electro Oy, developed the first wireless, portable heart rate monitor and changed forever the way athletes in aerobic sports trained. A wireless heart rate monitor has two components. The chest strap has built-in sensors that pick up the electrical activity of the heart and then send the signal from a small radio transmitter to a receiver worn on the wrist like a watch. Besides displaying your heart rate, most receivers also include time of day and a stopwatch and have a memory function to record lap times and heart rate by zones.

Basic models that only display heart rate start at about $50. If you want all of the bells and whistles plus the ability to download and manipulate data on your computer, expect to pay $400 or more. All types are available in triathlon, bike, running, and sporting goods stores, and through catalogs.

You don't have to use a heart rate monitor when training for your first triathlon, but it can help in getting intensity right during workouts. The training plan in Chapter 9 lists swim, bike, and run workouts to be used during training for your first triathlon. These workouts indicate how intense the effort should be using a scale of 1 to 5, with 5 being hardest. With a heart rate monitor you will know exactly what your intensity is. Without the monitor you will have to decide subjectively. This subjective rating is called "Rating of Perceived Exertion" (RPE) and is used if you *don't* have a heart rate monitor. The RPE zones used in your Chapter 9 training plan are as follows:

Zone 1   Very easy with light breathing

Zone 2   Easy with increased breathing

Zone 3   Moderately hard with somewhat labored breathing

Zone 4   Hard with labored breathing

Zone 5   Very hard with panting

Should you decide to buy a heart rate monitor, there are two basic ways you can determine what your heart rate zones are. First, you can go to a lab or clinic to be tested. In fact, this is a good idea even if you don't have a heart rate monitor. Not only will a "stress test" administered by a professional give you heart rate data, but it will also confirm that your heart is healthy and ready for training. This is something triathletes should each do periodically whether they use a heart rate monitor or not. Such a test generally costs $150 or more. Go to www.yourfirsttri.com to find more information on such testing and the locations of some test centers.

What you want to find out from such testing, other than fitness status, is your lactate threshold (sometimes called "anaerobic threshold") heart rate (LTHR). You're likely to test in only one sport—bike or run—but you can estimate the one not tested. If you ran on a treadmill, subtract eight beats per minute from the lactate threshold heart rate (LTHR) to estimate bike LTHR. If the test was done on a bike ergometer, add 8 beats per minute to estimate run LTHR.

The second way to determine your heart rate zones is to do what's called a "field test." This is a workout you do on your own out in the real world, not in a lab, and of course it's free. See the sidebar "Your Heart Rate Zones" for an explanation of how to do this. If you did the lab test, also use this sidebar to determine your personal zones.

While it's possible to use a heart rate monitor while swimming, don't do so unless you are an experienced swimmer. Remember that your purpose in the pool for now is to develop good swim form, not fitness. The latter will come as a

---

▶ YOUR HEART RATE ZONES

When using a heart rate monitor during exercise, the key is having a standard with which your target heart rate can be compared. I like to use lactate threshold heart rate (LTHR) for this marker. To find yours for running, go to a track, and after warming up for ten minutes, start running slowly around it. Every half lap (200 meters), increase your speed just a little, paying close attention to your breathing and effort. When you first notice the onset of rapid and deep breathing while experiencing a feeling of hard effort, look at your heart rate monitor. Your heart rate then is pretty close to your LTHR.

A similar method can be used to find your LTHR for the bike. On a long, gradual hill or stretch of flat road without stop signs, start riding easily and increase the effort every thirty seconds. When you first start to breathe rapidly and deeply, look at your heart rate monitor. The number is close to your LTHR.

Another way of gauging LTHR during a run or bike workout is to rate how hard you are running or biking on a scale of 1 to 5, with 5 being the hardest. Your LTHR is about 4 on this scale.

Once you know your LTHR in each sport, you can determine your five heart rate training zones. Here's how:

Zone 1. This is the easiest zone. You will spend a lot of time in the first zone warming up, on very easy days, and cooling down. If you are new to running, zone 1 will probably be walking. On the bike, zone 1 is like walking on your bike—very easy.

continued ➔

Your Heart Rate Zones *(continued)*

- My run zone 1 is less than _____ beats per minute (subtract 24 bpm from run LTHR)
- My bike zone 1 is less than _____ beats per minute (subtract 31 bpm from bike LTHR)

Zone 2. This is the aerobic training zone, the one you will use to improve your basic endurance and aerobic fitness. For the running newbie, zone 2 is slow jogging. For biking you're just starting to push the pedals a bit.

- My run zone 2 is _____ – _____ (15 to 23 bpm below run LTHR)
- My bike zone 2 is _____ – _____ (17 to 30 bpm below bike LTHR)

Zone 3. Use this zone only occasionally in workouts to improve race pace. When running or biking, this is when you first start to feel uncomfortable, but you know you could keep going for a long time.

- My run zone 3 is _____ – _____ (7 to 14 bpm below run LTHR)
- My bike zone 3 is _____ – _____ (10 to 16 bpm below bike LTHR)

Zone 4. This is a very hard effort, which you will not use at the beginning. But some day, after you become an experienced triathlete, you will use this zone, especially when preparing for sprint- and Olympic-distance races.

- My run zone 4 is _____ – _____ (1 to 6 bpm below run LTHR)
- My bike zone 4 is _____ – _____ (1 to 8 bpm below bike LTHR)

Zone 5. Above LTHR is zone 5—redline effort. Do not use this zone at all, as the risk of injury is greatly increased here and recovery after a workout takes much longer. Even after you are experienced in the sport there is little need to train this intensely.

- My run zone 5 is above _____ beats per minute (run LTHR)
- My bike zone 5 is above _____ beats per minute (bike LTHR)

result of working on your skills. But if you are an experienced swimmer, you can subtract 8 beats per minute from your bike LTHR to estimate swim LTHR and then set up zones (see the sidebar "Your Heart Rate Zones").

POWER METERS

Power meters are fairly recent additions to the triathlete's equipment arsenal, having been around only since the early 1990s. Whereas a heart rate monitor tells you what your body is doing (input), a power meter tells you what you are accomplishing (output). You might ask why you couldn't simply look at the speedometer on your handlebar computer to know what your output is. The problem with speed is that it is tremendously affected by outside influences such as wind and hills. If, for example, you told me that you completed a bike ride at an average speed of 18mph, I wouldn't know what that meant. If it was all downhill with a tailwind, that would have been a pretty low output. The same ride done uphill or into a strong headwind, however, could have been quite an accomplishment. The same problem applies whether you are drafting another triathlete or riding by yourself. Speed is just not a good measuring tool of output on the bike.

What power tells us is how much work you did per unit of time. Wind, hills, and drafting have no effect on it. If you told me you completed a ride at an average of 180 watts of power I would know exactly what that meant regardless of any other outside factors. As of this writing five types of power meters are available. Because this is a rapidly changing market, you should consult the manufacturer Web sites for more information.

SRM (www.srm.de)

This was the first commercially available power meter. It is made in Germany and is generally considered the top of the line. It is also the most expensive, starting at about $2,000. To use SRM you have to replace the crankarms and chainrings on your bike.

Power-Tap (www.cycle-ops.com)

The second power meter developed for cyclists, the Power-Tap costs considerably less (base price about $1,000) and opened the door for many more users. This power measuring device is built into your bike's rear hub.

ergomo (www.ergomo.de)

As are the SRM and Power-Tap, the ergomo is highly accurate and produces data similar to what is produced by the first two meters. This device is built into the bottom bracket on your bike. It costs about $1,200.

Polar S-720i (www.polarusa.com/consumer/powerkit/)

Polar, the company that started and still dominates the heart rate monitor business, got into the power meter fray in about 2001 with a unit that can be worn on your wrist for running and on the handlebars to display power. Heart rate is available in both uses (heart rate is also built into the previous three devices). The power meter doesn't directly measure power but rather estimates it based on chain tension. The price is about $300—far cheaper than the others— but it is somewhat less accurate.

CompuTrainer (www.racermateinc.com/computrainer.asp)

This is the "Cadillac" (if that's still a good term to use nowadays) of indoor, stationary bicycle trainers. In some ways it could be considered the first power meter, since it's been around since the 1980s. But it can't be used on the roads— only indoors. It has lots of other features besides power measurement and costs about $1,400.

GPS DEVICES

This is the latest cool addition to the high-tech triathlete's arsenal. Using the government's Global Positioning Satellites (GPS), these wristwatch-type devices allow you to not only keep track of where you are on the planet but also compute your real-time pace or speed, distance traveled, elevation, and hill gradients. They are especially helpful to use while running, since without such a device you have no idea what your pace is other than by guessing or running on a track while constantly translating lap splits into pace. A GPS device can also be used on your bike in place of the handlebar computer and will give you all of the same information and more—time, current speed, average speed, distance, elevation, and hill grade. Some also tell you heart rate. And they don't care if you are on a winding trail or a major thoroughfare, in the desert or downtown, climbing a mountain or along the seashore.

> **A GPS device is especially helpful while running, since without such a device you have no idea what your pace is other than by guessing or running on a track while constantly translating lap splits into pace.**

So long as you can see the sky, it's working and telling you what you're accomplishing (or not accomplishing). Starting at $160, these are a great value. Following are the endurance sport GPS devices available for purchase as of this writing. Again, please check with manufacturers for the most current information.

Timex Speed & Distance (www.timex.com/bodylink)

This was the first GPS for athletes. Over the years it has become more sleek and elegant. Besides the standard GPS data, it can also monitor heart rate. With the Timex S&D you wear a watch that displays data and a "Bodylink" sensor on an armband, clipped to your belt, or in your jersey pocket, which stores information for later transfer to your computer. Without heart rate the price is about $250. With heart rate it retails for about $275.

Garmin Forerunner (www.garmin.com/outdoor)

Garmin, the leader in the field of GPS for consumers, has two models available for endurance athletes—the original 201 and the 301. The most significant difference is that the 301 measures and displays heart rate during your workouts. Otherwise, they provide the basic GPS data explained above. The list price on the 201 is $160. The 301 lists for $325. They require wearing only a lightweight but somewhat oversized wristwatch. No other devices are worn (other than a chest strap for heart rate).

Suunto X9 (www.suunto.com)

At $699, this is the most expensive of the units described here. Although it doesn't have a heart rate function, it is the most elegant, with a handsome and lightweight design. It looks like a nice wristwatch rather than a clunky training tool. Besides the standard GPS features, it also has a barometer with weather-trend graphing and temperature.

BACK TO THE FUTURE

Someday all of these devices will be combined. We may even see the data display for them built into sunglasses, with a heads-up display on the lens similar to what fighter pilots have in their cockpits so they don't have to take their eyes off where they are going. That would be pretty cool!

Really serious athletes may eventually have a tiny chip medically imbedded to monitor heart rate, blood sugar, blood sodium, body acidity, velocity, elevation, distance, and gradient, all while predicting performance outcome. All of the data would be transmitted to a heads-up sunglasses display or to an earpiece and might even be presented as a single number called "Rating of Perceived Exertion." We'd then be right back where we started, only in a high-tech way. That's fun stuff for techies to ponder.

Chapter 11

YOUR FIRST TRIATHLON

Triathlon's active lifestyle is fun and rewarding, but the races can be a bit intimidating, perhaps even downright scary. And the closer you get to race day, the scarier it can become. The mere thought of the race may cause your heart to beat a little faster and give you an uneasy feeling. Why is this? Why is it you can swim, bike, and run with friends or alone and never feel anything but joy, yet become anxious, nervous, and apprehensive when going to or even thinking about a triathlon? The reason is that we each have a fear of the unknown and a fear of failure.

The best way to get control of your fear, even if it doesn't completely go away, is through self-confidence. Remind yourself that you're doing everything you can to get in shape and making good progress. Also, the more you know about what to expect at the race, the less intimidating race day becomes. This chapter gives you clear expectations for not only the race itself but also the days and final hours leading up to it.

You're likely to still be a bit edgy the last few days before your first triathlon. All triathletes are that way, even those who have been doing it for years. After all, this is *the* test. It's what you've been preparing to do for many, many weeks. No one wants to do poorly, and you won't if your race day attitude is right. You need to go to the start line with a calm demeanor, confident that you have done the homework and you're ready to go. Let's race!

CHOOSING AND ENTERING A RACE

Choosing the right first race is as important as training for it. By now you have probably already selected and entered one. Hopefully it's a pool-swim, sprint-distance race in your hometown, so that you know the course or at least have the opportunity to see and perhaps practice on it. That will give you a bit of a psychological boost and reduce the uneasiness you would otherwise feel on race day.

If you haven't selected one yet, Appendix H provides a list of sprint-distance races around the United States. For an updated listing of USA Triathlon–sanctioned events, go to www.USATriathlon.org and click on "Calendar." Then enter "sprint" in the search engine to bring up a list of all sprint-distance races sanctioned by USAT.

> If you need one you can get a license good for either the entire season or only race day. The seasonal license is the way to go if you think you'll do more than one race this year.

You can sign up for many of these races online, and a link is provided to each on the USAT calendar page. For others you may have to go to local registration sites such as a triathlon store or mail in your registration form.

All of the races in Appendix H require a USA Triathlon racing license. Some small local events that aren't USA Triathlon–sanctioned don't require a license. If you need one you can get a license good for either the entire season or only race day. The seasonal license is the way to go if you think you'll do more than one race this year. You can get it at the USA Triathlon Web site, or perhaps at the time of registration. Race-day-only licenses are always available from the race director. In either case, this will be made clear when you register.

Now let's look at what to do in the last few days before your first triathlon.

RACE WEEK

During the week of the race you may feel a bit strange because you'll be cutting back on exercise quite a bit to allow for rest. Although the extra time you'll have this week feels good, it can also make you a bit uneasy and even anxious. You'll probably feel you aren't doing enough and that your hard-earned fitness is fading away. Be rest assured that it isn't. In fact, you are gaining fitness by backing off this week. It's only during periods of low activity that the body gets stronger, by adapting to the stresses placed on it by the preceding higher levels of exercise. I've seen many triathletes, including very experienced ones who should know better, ruin their chances for good races by doing too much the week of their triathlons. Take it easy this week and fight off the self-doubt that tells you to do more. You'll do best by resting.

If you're following a training plan in Chapter 9, you'll find that your daily exercise has been reduced considerably. It's best to keep the rest of your week as much as possible like normal until the day before the race. This includes meals, sleep, work, and other activities.

The Day Before

If the race is in your hometown or close by, the day before won't be too unusual. You'll sleep in your own bed and eat from your own kitchen. That can be quite an advantage in keeping anxiety at bay. If you have to travel to the race, this is the day most people do it, although it's not necessarily the best from a racing perspective. Planning to arrive two days before would be better because it keeps stress levels lower. But you may be unable to fit that around your job and other responsibilities.

Today's Workout

This morning do a short workout. The training plan suggested in Chapter 9 calls for a bike ride to give you one last chance to make sure everything is working. Should there be some little mechanical problem, you've still got time to get it to a bike shop. If everything is in good order after the ride, it's still wise to check all bolts to make sure they are snug. Don't overtighten them; you may break or strip a bolt. Just ensure that nothing is loose.

A few sprint-distance triathlons require you to check your bike in the day before the race. Be sure to plan a morning ride well before the check-in time if this is a requirement of your triathlon.

Packet Pickup

More than likely you will have to pick up your race packet today. Bigger races often tie this in with an expo where vendors display their wares. It can be fun to see what is available for triathletes. Just be careful not to spend too much time on your legs; you want to rest them as much as possible today.

The packet will probably contain your race number or numbers, a course map with directions, comments on the rules of racing a triathlon (be sure to read this), a diagram of the transition area, start times by age group or ability, and sponsor information. The race number usually has a perforated portion with your name, age, and, perhaps, other identification. Check this to make sure it's correct before leaving the expo area.

You may also find a timing chip in the packet. This is a small electronic device that fastens to your ankle and identifies you. It is used to keep track of where you are on the course and your "splits"—the times of the individual swim, bike, and run legs of the race. Be sure to follow the instructions about how to wear your race chip exactly.

Know the Course

Even if you are familiar with the race course, today is a good time to drive it again to see if anything has changed. If you're from out of town and have never seen the course, this is imperative. Race directors almost always paint arrows on the road at all of the turns, so with a course map and by watching for the arrows you should be able to find your way easily. Even though there are likely to be lots of other racers and course marshals to direct you on race day, it's still your responsibility to know the route. Pay close attention to where hills and dangerous intersections are. Police should be on hand to control traffic for the race, but it's still a good idea to know what to expect.

Race Briefing

At this meeting, usually held on this day before the race, the race organizers explain what will happen on race day, including details about any changes to the course, how the transition area is set up, and any other last-minute updates. You can also expect to hear a lot of questions from nervous athletes. If there is such a meeting for entrants, you should attend even if it is not required.

Before you leave home, check the race information (online or in a packet mailed to you) to find out when and where the race briefing will be held. Arrive well in advance to allow time to check into your hotel and get to the meeting in an unhurried way. You will want to keep everything you do today as relaxed and unhurried as possible.

Eating and Drinking

You may need to change your diet a bit today to help prevent an upset stomach at the race. Breakfast can be your normal fare, but for the remainder of the day it may be best to avoid fibrous foods and

Endurance athletes tend to go overboard drinking fluids the day before a hot race. You're not a camel, so you won't be able to store huge amounts of fluid.

to eat lighter than usual. Soft foods (such as a baked potato), soup, or other liquid food sources are good choices for the night before your first triathlon.

Endurance athletes tend to go overboard drinking fluids the day before a hot race. You're not a camel, so you won't be able to store huge amounts of fluid. You'll simply pee more and are likely to dilute your electrolytes by drinking copious amounts. Just drink enough to quench your thirst.

Some triathlons offer a carbo-loading or pasta party the night before the race. This can be a fun experience, and you'll meet lots of other triathletes there. Again, expect almost everyone to be nervous and uptight. Don't let their concerns and agitation get to you. Remain calm and relaxed even if others around you are frazzled.

Race Gear Preparation

The evening before your race is a good time to get all of the stuff you'll need on race day organized and ready to go. Start by laying out all of your swim gear together. Make a second grouping of your bike gear minus the bike. Then put all of the run equipment together. Double-check your lists to make sure you have everything (see Appendix G).

Fasten your race number to your shirt or race belt and put it on to make sure it complies with the race director's instructions about how to wear it. They usually require a number on your back (and on the bike) during the bike portion and on your front during the run. If this is the case and they gave you only one number to wear on your body, an elastic race belt is the answer.

If there is only one transition area for your race, put all of your gear, along with your timing chip, in a bag or backpack to be carried to the race the next morning. But leave your swimsuit out, because you'll wear it to the race. If there are two transition areas (it's best not to do such a race for your first triathlon), pack two separate bags, making double sure you have only swim and bike gear in one and run stuff in the other.

Check the weather forecast for your race. That will help you decide what other clothes to take with you, such as sweats, arm covers, gloves, a raincoat, an umbrella, or various other warm-, cold-, or wet-weather gear. In general, I recommend taking more clothes than you think are necessary. I've seen race day weather unexpectedly turn nasty, catching athletes by surprise. The worst thing that could happen if you take extra clothes is that you'd have to carry them in and out of the transition area on race day. Load the extra clothes into a separate backpack, which may wind up staying in the trunk of the car tomorrow. But at least you know you have them just in case.

Keep Your Mind Off the Race

If you traveled to the race early and have a lot of time to kill today, it's best to stay away from other entrants so you can keep your mind off the race. Also, stay off your legs once you've done your morning workout (more on this shortly). Read a book, watch television, or go to a movie. If you're in a city you haven't visited before, another fun and relaxing option is to sign up for a bus tour of the area. The hotel can help you find such a service.

Sleep

Go to bed tonight at about your normal time or slightly earlier. If you're in a strange bed and a different time zone, especially if you traveled east, this may be a bit difficult. To help you get sleepy, turn the lights down low an hour or so before bedtime, read a book, or watch TV. Now is not the time to party with other triathletes.

RACE DAY!

The big day is finally here! The culmination of weeks of focused preparation has arrived. You're nervous, but that's normal. If you weren't a bit anxious that would be something to be concerned about. I like to see the athletes I coach just a bit on edge on race day. That means they'll be in the right frame of mind and race well.

Avoid thinking about what your finishing time will be or how you will place in your age group. Stop worrying about finishing last—you won't! Avoid undue pressure to perform today. With the possible exception of your mother, no one expects you to win the race. You're out there to have fun and just finish. So relax and enjoy the experience. There's nothing else like it in the world of sport.

Sleeping, Eating, and Other Problems

You may not have slept much, if at all, the night before. That's pretty common for triathletes at all levels. Don't let it concern you. If you slept satisfactorily two nights before, your race will still go well. Get up an hour or so before you have to

161

drive to the race venue but no less than three hours before your start time. That will allow you to wake up, perhaps drink a cup of coffee, eat a light breakfast, get dressed, and use the bathroom.

Your race day breakfast should have either been brought with you from home or purchased at a grocery the day before. The food you eat today should be easily digested as your stomach is likely to be squeamish. It's also a good idea to eat only foods you have eaten before workouts. It's generally not a good idea to do anything today that you haven't tried before in training.

Some foods that may go down easily for you today are unsweetened applesauce, banana, sports food supplements (such as GatorPro), liquid meals in a bottle (such as Ensure), and energy bars with water. Baby food is also easy to digest. Triathletes use a wide variety of foods before races; hopefully you have experimented with various foods before some of your workouts.

Assuming you're awake and up about three hours before your race start time, eat about 300 to 500 calories, depending on your size, appetite, and how nervous you feel. Don't skip breakfast today. A cup of coffee alone is not adequate to prepare your body for a triathlon.

Try to use the bathroom before leaving your room. Drinking hot coffee, tea, or even warm water as soon as you get up may help. This will be a lot more comfortable in your home or hotel than in a portable toilet at the race.

What to Wear

On the morning of the race, put on what you will wear for the swim portion of the triathlon. This may be a swimsuit or a one- or two-piece triathlon suit. You may want to wear some shorts and a T-shirt or sweatsuit over this. Check one last time to make sure you have your race numbers, timing chip, and swim, bike, and run gear before heading out the door.

Get There Early

Plan to arrive at the race venue 60 to 90 minutes before your start time. For some big races, 60 minutes may be cutting it close because of having to park and then walk to the transition area. You don't want to feel hurried and hassled. Allow enough time so that you can move at a leisurely pace and remain cool and calm. There are also a few things that must be done for race check-in, and these can take time.

Check-In

Triathlon check-in on race day may take 10 to 20 minutes. One of the first things you'll do is go through "body marking." This is usually right at the entrance to the transition area. A volunteer will ask to see your race number and then will use a marker to write the number on your arm and leg. Your age or age group code will also be written on your leg, usually on the calf. The race numbers identify you during the swim. The age mark lets your fellow triathletes know what age group you are in during the race.

If your bike wasn't checked in yesterday, a volunteer may need to do a safety check to make sure the handlebars are tight and the brakes work. Your helmet may also be checked to make sure it complies with U.S. Consumer Product Safety Commission (CPSC) safety standards for bicycle helmets (there should be a sticker inside that indicates this).

You're now ready to go into the transition area and rack your bike. The next order of business is to ensure that your tires are pumped up appropriately and to set up your personal transition space. If you don't have a pump, borrow one from another racer or race official. Bring your tire pressure up to about the level indicated on the sidewall of the tires. If it looks like it might rain or the pavement is wet, keep the tire pressure a little low.

The Transition Area

One of the things that makes triathlon such a unique sport is that the outcome is determined, in part, by how fast you can change from one sport to the next. This is called "transition" and is done in a special, usually fenced in, area for athletes only.

Following the swim you will hustle to the transition area to prepare for the bike portion of the race. This is called "transition #1" or "T1." After the bike ride you will come back to the transition area again and change equipment to start the run. This is "T2." Time spent in the transition area changing shoes, putting your helmet on or off, and doing everything else necessary to get out on the course again counts as a part of your total race time. The clock doesn't stop until you cross the finish line. For your first triathlon, don't be concerned about your time. But you do want your transitions to be smooth and efficient.

Since you are not allowed to have anyone help you, it's wise to organize your personal transition space and to rehearse your transitions several times in the final weeks before the race. The best time to rehearse T2 is when you do the combination or "brick" workouts described in Appendix E. T1 is a bit easier after a pool swim since there is no wet suit to mess around with after a cold-water swim, and you can rehearse this at any time; you should practice this at least a half dozen times before the race.

T1 and T2 are usually in the same area, but in a few races there may be two entirely different transition sites. This is rare for sprint-distance races but could be the case for yours. Be sure to find out well in advance. When the transitions are in different locations, often separated by a few miles, organizing them is more difficult and even more critical. It's easy to make a setup mistake. If, for example, your running shoes are placed at T1 or your helmet is at T2, you won't be able to continue and will be listed by the race director as a "DNF"—Did Not Finish.

Your Transition Stall

Your personal transition stall is often assigned by the race director. If it is, you will set up your transition stuff in that small, assigned space. If you are free to set up your stall wherever you want in the transition area, it is usually a good idea to locate it near the T1 exit—the place where you leave transition to head out

---

▶ TRANSITION CHECKLIST

Here is a checklist by transition area of all the equipment you must have or may want:

Transition #1 (swim-to-bike)

Bike___required

Helmet___required

Race number___usually required (may be on bike and/or a belt or pinned to shirt)

Bike shoes___optional (you can bike in running shoes, and many do)

Socks___optional (many triathletes race without them, but practice this first)

Sunglasses___optional

Water bottle with sports drink___optional, but a good idea

Cold weather gear___optional (gloves, jacket, arm covers, etc.)

Heart rate monitor chest strap___optional

T-shirt or singlet___often required

Towel___optional, but beneficial

Transition #2 (bike-to-run)

Running shoes___necessary (if you bike in them you're set)

Sunglasses___optional (may already be on from bike ride)

Race number___required (but may already be on shirt or belt)

Hat___optional

Note: Also refer to Appendix G on page 201.   ⊛

---

on the bike course. This is especially important if you will be wearing bike shoes instead of running shoes in the bike segment. In this location you can put your bike shoes on and then walk or run slowly with your bike to the exit where you can mount it, with minimal time spent jogging in clumsy bike shoes.

At the end of your bike ride, when you are approaching the transition and about 100 yards or so before you get there, slow down by coasting. If you have clipless pedals, you can save some time if you unfasten your shoes, and slip your feet out. Completely remove one first and then the other. Put your feet on the top of the shoes to finish pedaling easily to T2. Stop the bike and step off when instructed to do so. This will be just before the entrance to T2. Then you can run the bike to your stall barefoot with your shoes hanging from the pedals. This can be tricky, so be sure to practice before race day. This second run with your bike will be longer but easy without the clunky bike shoes on your feet. If you bike in running shoes, none of this is necessary, and you can set up your stall wherever it's convenient.

Transition Setup

Now let's take a look at how to organize your equipment at your personal transition stall. The transition area will generally have a simple bike rack made from pipes that looks like a big sawhorse or barricade. There are two ways you can put your bike on it. You can place the brake levers over the top of the rack so that it hangs from the handlebars with the front wheel off the ground, or you can place the nose of the saddle over the top of the rack so that the rear wheel is suspended. Either way is common, but the second may be necessary if you have some types of aerobars or if you're riding a mountain bike or other bike with flat or straight handlebars. The race director may even specify how it is to be racked. If so this will be in the instructions in your race packet or may be described at the pre-race meeting. Look around to see how others are racking their bikes.

Mount your water bottle, filled with the sports drink of your choice and ready to go, on your bike on race morning. You'll only need one such bottle on the bike. On the run there will be aid stations, so you won't need any bottles then.

Once your bike is racked, set up your transition stall. Start by spreading a bath towel on the ground on the opposite side of the bike from the chain. On this towel place your bike shoes (if you will be using these). Put them on the end of the towel farthest from the rack with the straps unfastened and as open as you can get them. If using running shoes instead, place them in the same manner.

On top of your shoes place your socks (if you will be using them). Most triathletes don't because it is difficult to put socks on wet feet. During your practices, try biking and running a few times without socks to see how you do. If you get hotspots or blisters on your feet, it's best to take a few seconds to put on socks in the transition. In this case find the socks that go on the easiest with damp feet. Try this a few times before race day.

Next, place your running shoes (if you don't ride in them) on the opposite end of the towel with the toes pointing away from you so you can slip into them easily. The laces should be loose and the tongue open wide for quick entry. This is where elastic laces or "quicklocks" come in handy, as tying shoes in transition can be clumsy. These lacing systems are inexpensive and can be purchased in most running and triathlon stores. They are worth the small cost. Trying to tie laces while breathing hard and in a hurry usually means the laces will soon come untied.

Place your running cap upside down on top of your running shoes so you can slap it on easily before putting on your shoes.

If you are using aerobars, lay your helmet upside down on the handlebars with the chin strap unclasped and the straps spread wide, with the front of the helmet pointing away from the rack. If you are not using aerobars, lay your helmet upside down on top of your hat and running shoes. In either case, place your sunglasses inside your helmet opened up, with the lenses down.

Lay the shirt you will wear on the bike and run on your saddle in such a way that you can slip it on. Make sure you find one that goes on easily when you are wet. Practice this several times in the last couple of weeks before the race.

It's not necessary, and may prove to be somewhat of a distraction, but if you're used to biking and running while watching your heart rate, you may want to wear your heart rate monitor in the triathlon; most triathletes do. If you want to, open the chest strap clasp and lay it on top of your shirt.

Most races require you to have a race number both on your bike and on your body throughout the bike and run. If there is a number to be placed on your bike, the race instructions will explain where it is to be mounted. If the race gives you two identical numbers to be worn on your body throughout the bike and run portions, you can pin these to your shirt front and back the night before. If they give you only one number, which is common, get a cheap, elastic, race belt with an easy-to-use clasp and safety pin the number to the middle portion of it that would normally be on your backside when the belt is worn. Start the bike leg of the race with the belt slid around so that the number is on your back where it can be seen easily by race officials. Then when you start the run you can simply slide the belt around your waist so that the buckle is on the back and the number is on the front, where race officials can once again easily see it as you're approaching the finish line. Again, be sure to try this belt several times when rehearsing T1 and T2.

If you wear a race number belt during the race, lay it on top of your sunglasses and helmet with the buckle unclasped.

The setup I've described here may sound overly structured, but I can tell you from experience that if you do it this way your race will be much smoother, as you'll know where everything is and there will be no fumbling. There is more panic and chaos during transition than at any other time in a triathlon. Most of this comes from those who are sloppy and unprepared. A bit of structure and some rehearsal will make the day much more fun for you.

Warm-Up

For your first triathlon you won't need much of a warm-up, if any at all. Assuming this is a pool swim, all lanes will probably be in use anyway, making it impossible to get a swim warm-up. Treat the race like a workout and start out slowly. Race directors seldom allow bikes out of the transition area before the race starts, and running really doesn't do much to prepare you for a swim. Since your purpose today is to enjoy and learn from the experience of finishing your first triathlon, starting the race slowly to warm up is not a problem. You'll simply do better today starting out this way rather than trying to be a rocket ship from the start.

The Start

Most triathlons start in waves, meaning small groups of athletes separated by a few minutes. In open-water swims the groups are usually determined by age. In pool swims predicted swim finish times are often used, since there will be two or more people in a lane and it makes things smoother if they are of similar ability. If so, your predicted swim time is generally asked for on the entry form. This should be based on times you get when practicing, especially the timed 400s called for every few weeks in the training plan in Chapter 9.

The race instructions should tell you when to report to the pool. When that time arrives, take your goggles with you to the swim check-in. You may also be required to wear a swim cap provided in your race packet.

The Swim

For a pool swim you will start in the water, holding on to the wall. If there are just two of you in a lane, you will probably be told to divide the lane in half, with each of you staying to your own side near the lane rope. If there are three or more in the lane, you'll swim a counterclockwise, circular pattern, always staying to the right side of the lane. Start slowly but steadily.

Be aware of the other swimmers in your lane if there are three in a lane. You're not trying to beat them, but you also don't want to hinder them. There is a certain etiquette that must be followed. The most important has to do with passing. If the swimmer behind touches your feet then, the next time you come to the wall, stay to the right, pause holding on to the wall, and allow him or her to pass. Then continue swimming.

In an open-water swim you may start either in the water or on the beach, running into the water at the starter gun. In either case, since this is your first triathlon, it's best to start in the back row and off to one side. Don't go to the middle of the front row. Open-water swim starts are notorious for how rough they are, especially in the front middle. Experienced triathletes describe this as like being in a washing machine with flying hands and elbows and kicking feet. It's not a fun place to be. Avoid it.

Don't be in a hurry during the swim. Do it just as you've done in swim practice—slow and steady. Stop whenever you feel like it. There is no penalty for stopping at any time in the race regardless of which leg of the event it is. In an open-water swim there will be boats, kayaks, or surfboards scattered along the course. Find one of these and hang on to it for a little while if you feel the need. You won't be the only one.

If it is a pool swim, a race official on deck will count your laps and tell you when it's time to stop. In an open-water swim you will follow buoys that mark the course; pause and look around occasionally to make sure you are on course. Coming to the end of your swim, you may find it a bit difficult to stand up and run to T1. You may be a bit wobbly and not have your land legs for a few seconds. So climb out of the pool and cautiously stand up, taking a moment to get your balance.

Transition #1

Walk or jog slowly from the water to your transition stall. With T1 laid out as described earlier in this chapter, making the switch from swim to bike should be a piece of cake. Pull on your socks (if applicable), slip into your shoes, put on your shirt and/or race number belt (with the number on your back), don your sunglasses, and plop on your helmet and buckle it. Then grab your bike off the rack and walk it to the bike exit. Be very careful if you have on bike shoes because they are rather clumsy to walk in. Once you're out of T1, a race official will tell you when you can mount your bike and start riding.

The Bike

Ride your bike just as you have done in practice dozens of times. Don't get into a head-to-head race with other triathletes. You're out here to have fun and finish the race; you're not here to beat someone or see how fast you can go. Save that for your second triathlon. Look around and enjoy the experience today. Shout words of encouragement to other triathletes.

There are a couple of rules you need to be aware of, which the race director probably discussed in the pre-race meeting yesterday. The first has to do with "drafting," which isn't allowed in your triathlon. Drafting is following closely be-hind another rider, which makes the going pretty easy and is considered an unfair advantage in a triathlon. Be sure to read about this in the race instructions and listen closely when the race director talks about it in the pre-race meeting. You may be penalized or disqualified for drafting.

The other rule has to do with "blocking." This means riding to the left side of the bike course, forcing others to pass you on the right side. In effect they are being blocked from passing you on the left side. The best way to avoid a penalty or being disqualified for blocking is to stay near the right curb except when passing.

Be sure to use your bottle of sports drink on the bike. For this race distance you won't need anything more. A couple of big sips every few minutes will keep you fueled all the way through the bike.

As you get close to the end of the bike course, sit up, slow down, and watch for course officials notifying you to get off your bike. About 100 yards or so before the finish, if you are wearing bike shoes, coast while you unfasten the straps and slip your feet out. Watch where you are going, and place your feet on top of the shoes by feel. Continue pedaling to the bike dismount area at the T2 entrance.

Transition #2

Approach T2 by gradually slowing down. Don't try to make up time or work hard to pass others in the last 100 yards. This can be a dangerous area if a lot of triathletes are finishing at the same time. Some will be going too fast, and others will be going so slow they are wobbly and weaving all over the road. Just ride a straight line and focus on what's happening ahead.

When an official tells you to dismount, come to a complete stop and get off your bike, leaving your bike shoes attached to the pedals. Then jog or walk with your bike to your transition stall. Rack your bike the same way it was when you came to T1. Step onto your towel and wipe your feet to remove any dirt or pebbles that may be stuck to them. Slip into your running shoes and cinch them up. Remove your helmet and grab your running hat (if applicable). If you are wearing a race belt, move your number to the front. Walk or run slowly to the exit from T2 where the run leg begins. This is generally *not* the same as where you came off the bike and entered T2. Be sure you know where this is before the race begins.

The Run

Head out onto the run course, paying close attention to how you feel. Should you find yourself breathing extraordinarily hard or have a higher heart rate than you're used to while running, slow down and walk for a while. Otherwise, continue to run slowly and steadily while watching for race officials, who will direct you through the course. Be aware that you may come to an intersection without an official or a police officer, so watch for signs or arrows on the road. Ultimately, you need to know the course.

When you come to an aid station there will be volunteers handing out cups of water and sports drinks. Walk through each aid station and take a cup of sports drink. Don't try to run and drink; just walk so you can get most of it down. Then continue running.

It's okay to walk at any time. This is your first triathlon, so enjoy it. There is no need to push yourself to your limits today. Look around and enjoy the experience of running in a triathlon with others who share your passion for health and fitness.

The Finish

As the finish line comes into view, you'll undoubtedly begin to speed up. Crossing under the finish banner, slow to a walk, and a race volunteer will direct you through the finish chute. At the end of the chute another race official will detach the perforated portion of your paper race number. These volunteers won't know what your time was. Your time and place overall and in your age group will be posted later on. It will be easy to tell where this posting is located, as there will be lots of triathletes crowding around that area looking for their results.

AFTER THE RACE

You did it! You finished your first triathlon and you're grinning ear to ear! But you don't really feel like celebrating much right now; you are tired and want to get off your legs. It's best to walk around for a few minutes to keep the blood moving and allow for a gradual cool-down. Five minutes or so should do it. You might walk over to where the post-race goodies are available for entrants and get something to eat and drink. If yo do not feel like eating much right now, look for a sports drink or eat something soft, like a banana. Getting in a few calories now will help you feel better later on.

Now you can go sit down with friends and family and tell them about your great experience. If you wore a stopwatch on your wrist during the race and pushed the lap button at the ends of the swim, bike, and run, you will be able now to recall the time splits for each leg of the race. You may be surprised to find that you went faster for each leg of the race than you had ever done in practice. It's amazing what extra rest leading up to a race and strong motivation on race day can do for performance.

Hang around afterward for the awards ceremony. It may not begin until an hour or so after you finish, but the wait for the ceremony is worth it. While you wait, try eating a bit. If your stomach is still a little queasy, don't force it down. Just continue taking in sports drinks. Once the ceremony begins, it goes quickly. Usually the top three in each age group are announced and called forward to receive their awards. When they come to your age group, listen for the times of the top finishers. It's amazing how fast the top triathletes are in each age group.

If you didn't get to see the official results, go to the race's official Web site the next day to find the posting. There you can find your name and see what your time splits were for each leg of the race. You might want to print this and keep it for future reference. As you move on in the sport, this will be your reference point. You're a triathlete now!

EPILOGUE

My nearly 3-year-old granddaughter, Keara, loves going to the swimming pool and riding her tricycle, and she runs everywhere with enthusiasm. None of these things are "practice" for her—they are who she is. She doesn't compartmentalize the things she does. I expect eventually she will learn to divide the day into hours, minutes, and seconds instead of seeing it all as fun. That's too bad. Life is most enjoyable when it's free-form. I think that's one of the reasons we look forward to our annual vacations—there are no, or at least fewer, constraints on how we spend our days. There is no routine.

Routines are not bad in and of themselves, however. If you followed a training plan in Chapter 9, that routine is what got you ready for your first triathlon. The typical triathlete's daily routine revolves around working out—perhaps even two or three times on some days. It takes some level of dedication to do this. Your nonathletic friends may already be amazed at your dedication to finishing a triathlon. If you are now fully hooked on triathlon, as I hope you are, then *they ain't seen nothin' yet.*

YOUR NEXT TRIATHLON

You've probably started thinking about your next race goal. That could be to do a sprint-distance triathlon faster. Or perhaps you're thinking about trying an Olympic-distance race (swim 1,640 yards, bike 24.8 miles, run 6.21 miles). Eventually you may even start entertaining thoughts of half-Ironman and Ironman triathlons (swim 2.5 miles, bike 112 miles, run 26.2 miles). Races such as these take more than six hours to finish (seventeen hours is the cutoff for Ironman) and should not be embarked upon lightly. I suggest you keep them in the back of your mind and occasionally compare where you are in the sport with what you think it will take to reach such a goal.

To achieve any of these triathlon goals will require you to not only follow a routine, but even be a bit obsessive about it, which will keep you on track for even greater fitness and self-fulfillment. But when we allow obsession to take the fun out of it, we diminish who we are. Swimming, biking, and running should be fun, not tasks to be completed and checked off. You should be following the triathlon lifestyle because you love it, not just because it's good for you.

THE TAO TRIATHLETE

The Chinese have a word for what they do in life that is fulfilling—"Tao," or the path. The Tao triathlete exercises and trains to be a better athlete, not to go faster. Faster comes with following the path of complete devotion and unwavering focus. The Tao archer spends hours completely focused on sending arrows at the target, not to see how many bull's-eyes he can make, but rather to better understand himself. The target is not an object related to scoring. It's a part of who he is.

Many triathletes want to "win" the workout. They do it only to beat their training partners or to push themselves to their limits—and then check it off in their training logs. Their youthful love for and fascination with the sport is eventually displaced by disdain. The Tao triathlete allows the workout to happen and sees the pool, bike path, and road merely as extensions of his or her life, to be accepted and enjoyed for what they are. Focusing externally on the clock or on others for every workout will eventually detract from the fun of exercise. Enjoyment and longevity in the sport come from making triathlon your lifestyle, not a mission to be accomplished.

CONSISTENCY AND MODERATION

Exercise is an end in itself. It is not merely a way of getting faster or going farther. These things will happen if you let them and are consistent. There will be days, however, when you just don't feel like swimming, biking, or running. That's to be expected and is part of what makes you human. Missing a workout does not mean you are no longer a triathlete. Frequently missing lots of workouts does. Consistency is key to fulfillment in triathlon.

The other key to fulfillment is moderation. Do not seek your physical limits on a daily basis. Rather, gently progress toward your goals with small steps. Doing otherwise results in injury, overtraining, illness, or burnout. Always. If one of these crops up it's because you were trying to *make* fitness happen rather than *allowing* it to happen.

THE NEW PATH

This book was only a tool in helping you finish your first triathlon. You are completely responsible for the achievement. You had to get yourself out of bed to do workouts while others slept. You changed the way you eat. You dedicated several hours a week to swimming, biking, and running. Your lifestyle has changed. In many ways you are now a new person—a triathlete.

You started reading this book to help you finish a triathlon. Now that you have done that, you can go back to your former lifestyle, or you can continue on the path you've started down. The choice is yours.

APPENDIX A: TRIATHLON LINGO

The following terms are used in books and magazines about triathlon and by triathletes in conversation.

Active recovery. A very easy workout intended to promote recovery from hard training. See also **Passive recovery**

Age group. A competitive division among the amateurs in a race, such as "female 30–34."

Age grouper. An amateur triathlete.

Aerobars. A type of bike handlebar that makes the rider more aerodynamic.

Body marking. The writing of your race number and age group on your arm and leg by a race volunteer before a triathlon.

Bonk. Extreme exhaustion, usually caused by using up most of the carbohydrates stored in your muscles.

BOP. A triathlete who usually finishes in the "back of the pack," or among the last of the entrants.

Brick. A continuous, combination workout including either the swim and bike or bike and run.

Cadence. Revolutions or cycles per minute of the swim stroke, pedal stroke, or run stride.

Cool-down. Low-intensity exercise at the end of a workout.

DNF. Abbreviation for "did not finish" in the race results.

Drafting. Swimming, biking, or running closely behind someone else to reduce effort.

Drops. The lower portion of turned-down handlebars.

Free weights. Weights that are not part of an exercise machine, such as barbells and dumbbells.

Frequency. The number of times per week that someone works out.

Half-Ironman. A triathlon with 1.2-mile swim, 56-mile bike, and 13.1-mile run portions.

Hammer. A fast, sustained effort.

Hamstring. The muscle on the back of your thigh that flexes the knee and extends the hip.

Hoods. On drop handlebars, the covers of the brake handles.

Intervals. A type of high-intensity exercise marked by short but regularly repeated periods of hard efforts separated by periods of recovery.

Ironman. A trademarked brand owned by the World Triathlon Corporation, referring to a triathlon with 2.4-mile swim, 112-mile bike, and 26.2-mile run portions.

Mash. To push a high gear on your bike.

MOP. A triathlete who usually finishes in the "middle of the pack" of entrants.

Newbie. Someone new to triathlon.

Olympic-distance race. A triathlon with 1,500-meter swim, 25-mile bike, and 6.2-mile run portions.

Passive recovery. A period of time with no workouts, intended to promote recovery from hard training; a day off from exercise. (See also **Active recovery**.)

Periodization. A method of sequentially organizing training to achieve a high level of fitness by the time of an important race.

PR. Abbreviation for "personal record"—someone's best time ever for a given swim, bike, or run distance; also sometimes referred to as "PB" for "personal best."

Quadriceps ("quads"). The large muscle in front of the thigh that straightens the knee and flexes the hip.

Repetition. The number of times a task, such as lifting a weight, is repeated.

RPM. Revolutions per minute. Same as cadence.

Set. A group of repetitions.

Singlet. A sleeveless shirt, often worn when running or biking.

Spinning. Pedaling at a high cadence or RPM.

Split. Someone's time for a given portion of the race, such as the bike split.

Sprint-distance race. A short triathlon with distances that are generally about 400–500 meters for the swim, 10–15 miles for the bike, and 3 miles for the run.

T1. Transition #1—the swim-to-bike transition.

T2. Transition #2—the bike-to-run transition.

Taper. A short period of time, generally a few days or one to two weeks, before an important race during which the amount of training done is reduced to increase rest, which produces greater fitness.

Transition. An area designated for changing from one sport to the next, such as from swim to bike (see **T1**) and bike to run (see **T2**).

Tops. The portion of the drop-down handlebars closest to the stem.

Warm-up. The period of gradually increasing intensity of exercise at the start of a workout.

Wave. A group of triathletes within a race who are started at the same time in order to prevent overcrowding on the course.

APPENDIX B: SWIM WORKOUTS

The intensity of the following workouts is determined by five zones of perceived exertion, based on your breathing and effort:

Zone 1   Very easy effort with comfortably light breathing

Zone 2   Easy effort with increased breathing volume

Zone 3   Moderately hard effort with somewhat labored breathing

Zone 4   Hard effort with labored breathing

Zone 5   Very hard effort with panting

The workouts are written so that yards or meters can be used, depending on your pool's measurement.

Swim Workout #1. This is a **10-minute** swim. Swim one length of the pool, concentrating on your swim stroke mechanics. The effort should be low (zones 1–2). Stop and rest at the wall for **30–45 seconds**. Then swim back to the other wall and rest again. Continue this for 10 minutes.

Swim Workout #2. This is a **15-minute** swim. Swim one length of the pool, concentrating on your swim stroke mechanics. The effort should be low (zones 1–2). Stop and rest at the wall for **30–45 seconds**. Then swim back to the other wall and rest again. Continue this for 15 minutes.

Swim Workout #3. This is a **15-minute** swim. Start by swimming as far as you can without stopping or allowing your stroke mechanics to break down, no longer than 400 yards/meters. Keep the effort low—zones 1 or 2. Rest for **1 minute** or so at the wall. For the remainder of the 15 minutes repeat the one length of the pool swim with good form in zones 2–3 with **30–45 seconds** of rest at the wall after each.

Swim Workout #4. This is a **15-minute** swim. Swim 100 yards/meters at zone 1, focusing on stroke mechanics. Rest **30–45 seconds**. Then swim 75 yards/meters with good form in zone 2. Rest **30–45 seconds**. Swim 50 yards/meters with good form in zone 2. Rest **30–45 seconds**. For the remainder of the 15 minutes, repeat the one-length swim with good form in zone 2, followed by **30–45 seconds** of rest at the wall after each.

Swim Workout #5. This is a **15-minute** swim. Swim 100 yards/meters at zone 1, focusing on stroke mechanics. Rest **30–45 seconds**. Then swim 25 yards/meters with good form in zone 3. Rest **30–45 seconds**. Do the 25-yard swim three more times with the same rest breaks. For the remainder of the 15 minutes repeat the one-length swim with good form in zone 1, followed by **30–45 seconds** of rest at the wall after each.

Swim Workout #6. Warm up by swimming 100 yards/meters in zone 1. Then swim 400 yards/meters nonstop in zones 2–3. Time yourself.

Swim Workout #7. Swim with your masters swim team. Ask the instructor on the deck for feedback on your technique. If no masters group is available, swim your own workout, always concentrating on good form.

Swim Workout #8. This is for the experienced swimmer. Warm up as follows: 50-yard/meter swim in zone 1, 50-yard/meter kick in zone 1, 100-yard/meter pull in zone 2, 100-yard/meter swim in zone 2. Then do four 100-yard/meter swims in zone 3 (10-second recoveries). Rest for **1 minute**. Then do four 100-yard/meter swims (10-second recoveries) with each one slightly faster than the previous one, but all below zone 5. Rest **1 minute**. Cool down with a 200-yard/meter, zone 1 swim. You may vary this workout by changing the four 100-yard/meter swims to eight 50-yard/meter swims, two 200-yard/meter swims, or some other pattern. Total: 1,300 yards/meters.

If you have questions about any exercise here, go to www.yourfirsttri.com for assistance.

APPENDIX C: BIKE WORKOUTS

The intensity of the following workouts is determined by five zones of perceived exertion, based on your breathing and effort:

Zone 1   Very easy effort with comfortably light breathing

Zone 2   Easy effort with increased breathing volume

Zone 3   Moderately hard effort with somewhat labored breathing

Zone 4   Hard effort with labored breathing

Zone 5   Very hard effort with panting

Bike Workout #1. This is a **20-minute** ride and is best done on a mostly flat course or on an indoor trainer. Gradually increase the intensity from zone 1 to zone 2 as you warm up. Stay mostly in zone 2 throughout the remainder of the ride. Concentrate on your pedaling cadence (count every time your right foot goes down for one minute). If on a flat stretch of road it is below 90 RPM, shift to a lower (easier) gear. On the road, every time you encounter a small hill or headwind, shift to a lower (easier) gear to maintain 90 RPM. Shift to a higher (harder) gear on downhills. If on an indoor trainer, play with the gears, shifting frequently, and notice how your cadence changes when you do. Cool down in zone 1 for **5 minutes**.

Bike Workout #2. This is best done on an indoor trainer, as it's a bit risky on the road. Ride for **20 minutes**. After a **5-minute** warm-up building from zone 1 to zone 2, unclip one foot from the pedal and place it on a chair or box next to the bike. Then, with the bike in a low and easy gear, pedal with the other leg. You'll find that at the top of the pedal stroke there is a "dead" spot that is a bit difficult to pedal through. Focus on this dead spot to smooth it out. At first you will last only a few seconds with one leg as it fatigues quickly. Change legs when this happens. Over time you will become more efficient at the top of the stroke and be able to pedal longer before tiring. This is a sign that your transitions are improving. Strive for **2 minutes** on a leg before needing to change legs. Allow **5 minutes** at the end for easy pedaling to cool down.

Bike Workout #3. Ride your bike for **30 minutes** on a mostly flat course or on an indoor trainer. After a **10-minute** warm-up, concentrate on the 9-to-3 drill. Think of the pedal stroke as being the face of a clock, with 12 o'clock at the top and 6 o'clock at the bottom. When the crankarms are parallel to the ground, the forward foot is in the 3 o'clock position and the back foot is at 9 o'clock. What you want to do in this drill is feel like you are moving your rear foot straight forward from 9 to 3 on the clock face without ever going through 12. Obviously you are, but by firing the muscles this way you train them to transition smoothly. Every minute or so, think about pedaling this way for several seconds. Take a mental break and then do it again. Repeat this frequently throughout the ride. Leave the last **5 minutes** for an easy cool-down in zone 1.

Bike Workout #4. Ride your bike for **40 minutes** on a mostly flat course or an indoor trainer. After a **10-minute** warm-up, concentrate on the shoe-top drill. As you are pedaling, try to keep your foot against the top inside of the shoe and avoid touching the bottom inside of the shoe. This drill emphasizes all parts of the pedal stroke except the downstroke, which is the easy part. Leave the last **10 minutes** for an easy cool-down in zone 1.

Bike Workout #5. Ride your bike for **40 minutes** on a mostly flat course or an indoor trainer. After a **10-minute** warm-up, concentrate on the toe-touch drill. As your foot approaches the 12 o'clock position, try to touch your toes to the front end of your shoe. Make sure your heel is slightly higher than the ball of your foot when doing this. Leave the last **10 minutes** for an easy cool-down in zone 1.

Bike Workout #6. Ride your bike for **40 minutes** on a mostly flat course or an indoor trainer. After a **10-minute** warm-up, concentrate on the spin-up drill. Shift to a lower (easier) gear and gradually increase your cadence for about **20 to 30 seconds** until you start to bounce on the saddle. At that point reduce your cadence slightly until you stop bouncing, and pedal as smoothly as you can for several seconds. Then shift to a higher (harder) gear and pedal normally for a few minutes. Repeat this drill several times. Over time your comfortable range will increase. Leave the last **10 minutes** for an easy cool-down in zone 1.

Bike Workout #7. Ride your bike for **30 minutes** on a mostly flat course or on an indoor trainer. After a **10-minute** warm-up, concentrate on the pedal-mash drill. Shift to a higher (harder) gear, one that keeps your cadence between 50 and 60 (you may need to count every time your right foot goes down to get this right). For **15 seconds**, stay seated and drive the pedals down with a lot of effort at this low cadence. Then shift back to a normal gear and pedal easily at a comfortably high cadence for **1 minute and 45 seconds**. Repeat this drill four more times. In other words, do one mash drill every **2 minutes**. *Do not do this drill if you have sensitive knees*. Instead, ride in zone 2 for **10 minutes**. Leave the last **10 minutes** for an easy cool-down in zone 1.

Bike Workout #8. Ride your bike for **30 minutes** on a course with lots of short hills. The experienced rider may make this a **60-minute** ride. After a **10-minute** warm-up, climb several hills, staying seated and keeping your cadence above 70 RPM (you may need to count every time your right foot goes down for 1 minute). A variation on this workout is to do three to five repeats on a hill that takes about 2 minutes to climb. *Do not do this workout if you have sensitive knees.*

Instead, ride in zone 2 for **10 minutes**. Leave the last **5–10 minutes** for an easy cool-down in zone 1.

Bike Workout #9. Ride your bike for **40 minutes** on a mostly flat course or an indoor trainer. Stay in zones 1 and 2 for the entire ride. Your cadence should be comfortably high.

Bike Workout #10. Ride your bike for **60 minutes** on a mostly flat course or an indoor trainer. Stay in zones 1 and 2 for the entire ride. Your cadence should be comfortably high.

Bike Workout #11. Ride your bike for **50 minutes** on a mostly flat course or an indoor trainer. After a **20-minute** warm-up building intensity from zone 1 to zone 2, ride for **20 minutes** steady in zone 3 (an experienced cyclist can do this in zone 4). Cool down in zone 1 for **10 minutes** at a high cadence.

Bike Workout #12. Ride your bike for **60 minutes** on a mostly flat course or an indoor trainer. After a **20-minute** warm-up building intensity from zone 1 to zone 2, ride for **30 minutes** steady in zone 3 (an experienced cyclist can do this in zone 4). Cool down in zone 1 for **10 minutes** at a high cadence.

Bike Workout #13. This is a workout for an experienced cyclist. Ride for **90 minutes** in zones 1 and 2 on a mostly flat course or indoor trainer.

Bike Workout #14. This is a workout for an experienced cyclist. Ride for **2 hours** in zones 1 and 2 on a mostly flat course or indoor trainer.

Bike Workout #15. This is a workout for an experienced cyclist. Ride for **60 minutes**. After about **10 minutes**, go to a moderate grade hill (4–6 percent grade) that takes **4–6 minutes** to climb, and do four repeats in the aero position. The coast-down time is your recovery. Keep your cadence above 80 RPM on the climbs. Cool down for a few minutes in zone 1.

If you have questions about any exercise here, go to www.yourfirsttri.com for assistance.

APPENDIX D: RUN WORKOUTS

The intensity of the following workouts is determined by five zones of perceived exertion, based on your breathing and effort:

Zone 1   Very easy effort with comfortably light breathing

Zone 2   Easy effort with increased breathing volume

Zone 3   Moderately hard effort with somewhat labored breathing

Zone 4   Hard effort with labored breathing

Zone 5   Very hard effort with panting

Run Workout #1. This is a **20-minute** walk-run session and is best done on a flat, soft surface such as gravel, grass, dirt, or a track. Avoid concrete and asphalt if at all possible. Warm up by walking briskly for **5 minutes,** increasing the intensity from zone 1 to zone 2 as you progress. Then alternate **15-second** runs with **45-second** walks, ten times. The walk portions are done in zone 1. The runs should be zone 3 intensity. Cool down by walking in zone 1 for **5 minutes**.

Run Workout #2. This is a **20-minute** walk-run session and is best done on a flat, soft surface such as gravel, grass, dirt, or a track. Avoid concrete and asphalt if at all possible. Warm up by walking briskly for **5 minutes,** increasing the intensity from zone 1 to zone 2 as you progress. Then alternate **30-second** runs with **30-second** walks, ten times. The walk portions are done in zone 1. The runs should be zone 3 intensity. Cool down by walking in zone 1 for **5 minutes**.

Run Workout #3. This is a **20-minute** walk-run session and is best done on a flat, soft surface such as gravel, grass, dirt, or a track. Avoid concrete and asphalt if at all possible. Warm up by walking briskly for **5 minutes,** increasing the intensity from zone 1 to zone 2 as you progress. Then alternate **60-second** runs with **30-second** walks, seven times. The walk portions are done in zone 1. The runs should be zone 3 intensity. Cool down by walking in zone 1 for about **5 minutes**.

Run Workout #4. This is a **20-minute** walk-run session and is best done on a flat, soft surface such as gravel, grass, dirt, or a track. Avoid concrete and asphalt if at all possible. Warm up by alternating **1 minute** of walking briskly in zone 1 with **1 minute** of running in zone 2 for a total of **5 minutes**. Then run **10 minutes** in zone 2. It's okay to stop and walk a few seconds if this seems harder than zone 2. Cool down by walking in zone 1 for **5 minutes**.

Run Workout #5. This is a **30-minute** walk-run session and is best done on a flat, soft surface such as gravel, grass, dirt, or a track. Avoid concrete and asphalt if at all possible. Warm up by alternating **1 minute** of walking briskly in zone 1 with **1 minute** of running in zone 2 for a total of **5 minutes**. Then run **3 minutes** in zone 2 and walk **1 minute** in zone 1. Do this five times. Cool down by walking in zone 1 for **5 minutes**.

Run Workout #6. This is a **30-minute** walk-run session and is best done on a flat, soft surface such as gravel, grass, dirt, or a track. Avoid concrete and asphalt if at all possible. Warm up by alternating **1 minute** of walking briskly in zone 1 with **1 minute** of running in zone 2 for a total of **5 minutes**. Then run **20 minutes** in zone 2. It's okay to stop and walk a few seconds if this seems harder than zone 2. If your race will be on a hilly course, do this workout on hills. It's okay to alternate walking and running on the hills. Cool down by walking in zone 1 for **5 minutes**.

Run Workout #7. This is a **30-minute** run and is best done on a flat, soft surface such as gravel, grass, dirt, or a track. Avoid concrete and asphalt if at all possible.

Run **30 minutes** in zone 2. It's okay to stop and walk a few seconds if it seems harder than zone 2 at times. If your race will be on a hilly course, do this workout on hills. It's okay to alternate walking and running on the hills. How much distance did you cover in **30 minutes**?

Run Workout #8. This is about a **20-minute** "strides" workout and is best done on a flat, soft surface such as gravel, grass, dirt, or a track. Parks are excellent for this workout. Do not do this workout on concrete and asphalt. Warm up by alternating **1 minute** of walking briskly in zone 1 with **1 minute** of running in zone 2 for a total of **7 minutes** (the experienced runner can run for **15 to 20 minutes**, building from zone 1 to zone 2). Then on a flat or very slightly downhill course that is approximately 100 yards long, run **20 seconds** in zone 4. Note that these are *not* zone 5 (all-out effort). Hold back and concentrate on running form, not speed. Count each time your right foot touches the ground for this **20 seconds**. The number should be at least 29. Turn around and walk back to your starting point. Do four to six of these strides. If you are taking fewer than 29 right-foot steps in **20 seconds,** shorten and quicken your stride without running any harder than zone 4. As a variation on this workout, do the first two or three strides barefoot (on grass only, and be sure to check for sharp objects first). When you put your shoes back on, try to run with the same good form you used when barefoot. Cool down by walking in zone 1 for **5 minutes**. The experienced runner can vary this workout by doing the strides uphill and may extend it to **45 minutes,** with a longer warm-up and cool-down.

Run Workout #9. This is a workout for an experienced runner. Run **30 to 45 minutes,** building from zone 1 to zone 2 while concentrating on good form with a high cadence (at least 28 right-foot strikes in **20 seconds**).

Run Workout #10. This is a workout for an experienced runner. Run **60 minutes.** In the first **30 minutes,** build intensity from zone 1 to zone 2. Run the last **30 minutes** in zone 3.

Run Workout #11. This is a workout for an experienced runner. Run **45 minutes** total. The first **10 minutes** is warm-up, building from zone 1 to zone 2. Then on grass or a track, run **3 minutes** at your current 5K race pace, five times, with **3-minute** recovery intervals. Cool down with an easy run in zone 1.

Run Workout #12. This is a workout for an experienced runner. Run **60 to 75 minutes,** building from zone 1 to zone 2 while concentrating on relaxed running form.

If you have questions about any exercise here, go to www.yourfirsttri.com for assistance.

APPENDIX E: COMBINATION WORKOUTS

The intensity of the following workouts is determined by five zones of perceived exertion, based on your breathing and effort:

Zone 1   Very easy effort with comfortably light breathing

Zone 2   Easy effort with increased breathing volume

Zone 3   Moderately hard effort with somewhat labored breathing

Zone 4   Hard effort with labored breathing

Zone 5   Very hard effort with panting

While combining workouts, remember that this is a good time to practice your transition area. See page 164.

Combination Workout #1. Bike for **30 minutes** on a mostly flat course or an indoor trainer. Gradually increase the intensity from zone 1 to zone 2 as you warm up. Stay mostly in zone 2 throughout the remainder of the ride. Quickly transition to a **10-minute** run or walk-run on a flat course in zones 1 to 2.

Combination Workout #2. Bike for **40 minutes** on a mostly flat course or an indoor trainer. Gradually increase the intensity from zone 1 to zone 2 as you warm up. Stay mostly in zone 2 throughout the remainder of the ride. Quickly transition to a **10-minute** run or walk-run on a flat course in zones 1 to 2.

Combination Workout #3. Bike for **50 minutes** on a course that is similar to the bike course in your first triathlon or on an indoor trainer. After a **20-minute** warm-up building intensity from zone 1 to zone 2, ride for **30 minutes** steady in zone 3 (an experienced cyclist can do this in zone 4). Quickly transition to a **10-minute** run or walk-run on a flat course in zones 1 to 2.

Combination Workout #4. Bike for **50 minutes** on a course that is similar to the bike course in your first triathlon or on an indoor trainer. After a **20-minute** warm-up building intensity from zone 1 to zone 2, ride for **30 minutes** steady in zone 3 (an experienced cyclist can do this in zone 4). Quickly transition to a **20-minute** run or walk-run on a flat course in zones 1 to 2.

If you have questions about any exercise here, go to www.yourfirsttri.com for assistance.

APPENDIX F: STRENGTH WORKOUTS

Strength Workout #1: AA Phase. The purpose of the AA phase is to perfect the exercise movements while building general body strength. Warm up by spinning on a stationary bike for **5 minutes**. Then with a **30RM load** (a weight you could only lift about 30 times), do **3 sets** of **20 reps** each (it will feel easy) of the following exercises: (a) leg press; (b) seated row; (c) chest press; (d) heel raise or knee extension or leg curl (choose one of these three based on your personal weakness—calf, knees, hamstrings); (e) abdominal curl with twist; and (f) standing, bent-arm, and lat pull down. Complete all three sets before advancing to the next exercise. Focus on doing each exercise with perfect form. Form is more important than weight loads in this phase. Cool down by riding a stationary bike for **5 minutes** with a high cadence and a low resistance.

Strength Workout #2: MT Phase. The purpose of the first two workouts in the MT phase is to transition from lighter to heavier loads. This is the first week of the MT phase. Warm up by spinning on a stationary bike for **5 minutes**. Then with a **20RM load** (a weight you could only lift about twenty times), do **3 sets** of **15–20 reps** each. Stop each set when you feel you could only lift the weight one or two more times. Do *not* go to failure. Do the following exercises: (a) leg press; (b) seated row; (c) heel raise or knee extension or leg curl (choose one of these three based on your personal weakness—calf, knees, hamstrings); (d) abdominal curl with twist; and (e) standing, bent-arm, and lat pull down. (*Note that the chest press exercise is not included now.*) Complete all three sets before advancing to the next exercise. Maintain good form on each rep. Cool down by riding a stationary bike for **5 minutes** with a high cadence and a low resistance.

Strength Workout #3: MT Phase. The purpose of the MT phase is to improve triathlon-specific movement strength. This is for all weeks of the MT phase after the first week. Warm up by spinning on a stationary bike for **5 minutes**. Then with a **15RM load** (a weight you could only lift about fifteen times), do **3 sets of 10–15 reps** each. Stop each set when you feel you could only lift the weight one or two more times. Do *not* go to failure. Do the following exercises: (a) leg press; (b) seated row; (c) heel raise or knee extension or leg curl (choose one of these three based on your personal weakness—calf, knees, hamstrings); (d) abdominal curl with twist; and (e) standing, bent-arm, and lat pull down. Complete all three sets before advancing to the next exercise. Maintain good form on each rep. Cool down by riding a stationary bike for **5 minutes** with a high cadence and a low resistance.

Strength Workout #4: SM Phase. The purpose of the SM phase is to maintain the strength you have built. Warm up by spinning on a stationary bike for **5 minutes**. Do only **2 sets** with **10–15 reps** of each exercise. The *first set* is done with a **20RM load** (a weight you could lift 20 times). The *second set* is with a **15RM load** (a weight you could lift fifteen times). Stop the second set when you feel you could only lift the weight one or two more times. Do *not* go to failure. Do the following exercises: (a) leg press; (b) seated row; (c) heel raise or knee extension or leg curl (choose one of these three based on your personal weakness—calf, knees, hamstrings); (d) abdominal curl with twist; and (e) standing, bent-arm, and lat pull down. Complete all sets before advancing to the next exercise. Maintain good form on each rep. Cool down by riding a stationary bike for **5 minutes** with a high cadence and a low resistance.

If you have questions about any exercise here, go to www.yourfirsttri.com for assistance.

APPENDIX G: CHECKLISTS

Following are lists of triathlon equipment that you will need or may want for your first triathlon.

You Must Have

____ Swimsuit, trisuit, or bike shorts (worn throughout the race)

____ Run and bike shirt (may be a T-shirt)

____ Swim goggles

____ Bike

____ Bike shoes (may be running shoes)

____ Bike helmet

____ Bike water bottle

____ Sports drink

____ Running shoes

____ Sunscreen

____ Race instructions

____ Race number (may be on bike and/or a belt or pinned to shirt)

It Would Be Good If You Had

____ Wet suit (if open-water swim)

____ Aerobars on bike

____ Handlebar computer

____ Lace locks or elastic laces on shoes

____ Race belt for attaching number (may be pinned to shirt instead)

____ Bike pump

____ Wrist stopwatch/heart rate monitor (with chest strap)/GPS

___ Transition towel

___ After-race clothing

___ Sunglasses

___ Cold weather gear (gloves, jacket, arm warmers, etc.)

It Might Help If You Had

___ Running shorts to wear over swimsuit on bike and run

___ Nose plugs and earplugs for swimming

___ Running hat

___ Nonstick cooking spray to help slip wet suit off (open-water swim)

___ Plastic bag to carry wet swim stuff home

___ Spare pair of swim goggles

___ Windbreaker for biking in case it's cold

___ Toilet paper

___ Plastic bag to cover saddle (in case of rain)

___ Transition stall marker (for example, balloon or ribbon)

___ Socks (rolled down for easy entry in T1)

If Traveling Overnight to a Race You Need

___ Nonperishable breakfast foods

___ Personal pillow (if driving to race)

APPENDIX H: NEWBIE-FRIENDLY RACES

The following are novice-friendly triathlons around the United States. They are listed in the order in which they occurred within each state in 2005. Go to the listed Web sites for more details. Check with local triathlon, swimming, biking, running, and sporting goods stores for other sprint-distance races in your region.

Arizona

Deuces Wild Tri Festival Sprint, www.trisportsracing.com

Mountain Man Triathlon Sprint, www.mountainmanevents.com

Arkansas

Degray Lake Sprint, www.dltmultisport.com

Cats Sprint, tri www.catstri.org

California

UCSB Spring Sprint Triathlon, www.ucsbtriathlon.org

Bakersfield Triathlon Sprint, www.bakersfieldtriathlon.com

Wildflower Sprint, www.tricalifornia.com

San Jose Mountain Bike Sprint, Triathlon, www.japroductions.com

Breath of Life Ventura Triathlon, Sprint, www.triforlife.com

Santa Cruz Triathlon—Sprint, www.bythebeachproductions.com

Donner Lake Sprint Triathlon, www.changeofpace.com

Santa Barbara Triathlon (women's sprint), www.santabarbaratriathlon.com

Santa Barbara Triathlon Sprint, www.santabarbaratriathlon.com

Tinley's Hot Road Bike Triathlon Sprint, www.tricalifornia.com

Tinley's Offroad Sprint Triathlon, www.tricalifornia.com

Windman Sprint, www.windmanevents.com

Colorado

Surf & Turf Aquathon, www.aquathonusa.com

Buffalo Creek Sprint Offroad Triathlon, www.youtriit.com

5430 Sprint Triathlon, www.5430sports.com

Denver Athletic Club Sprint Triathlon, www.denverathleticclub.org

Work Out West Endless Summer Sprint Tri, www.workoutwest.com

Surf & Turf Aquathlon USA Super Sprint, www.aquathonusa.com

Triamerica Vailavon Sprint, www.sommersports.com

Fall Frenzy Sprint Triathlon, www.fallfrenzy.com

Connecticut

Pat Griskus Sprint Triathlon, www.patgriskustri.com

Delaware

Sports Sprint Tri, www.races2run.com

Dewey Beach Sprint Triathlon, www.deweybeachtriathlon.com

Florida

Tri Gator Sprint Tri, www.trigator.com

TriAmerica Clermont Sprint, www.triamerica.com

Powerade Sprint Duathlon, www.familyfitnessweekend.com/
ffwcitiesstaugustine/index.asp

Tri Miami Triathlon Sprint, www.multirace.com/triathlon

Beaches Fine Arts Sprint Tri, www.bfastriathlon.org

Coca Cola Classic Sprint Tri Deerfield Beach, www.familyfitnessweekend.com

Powerade Sprint Du Deerfield Beach, www.familyfitnessweekend.com

Crystal River Sprint Tri, www.crtri.com

Powerade Sprint Duathlon Sarasota, www.familyfitnessweekend.com

Jaxtri Series Sprint, www.jaxtri.com

Crystal River Sprint Tri, www.crtri.com

Reebok Women's Tri St. Petersburg Sprint, www.reebokwomenstriathlon.com

Huntington's Disease Sprint Triathlon, www.huntingtonsdisease.fl.org

Deland Triathlon Sprint, www.buttar.com

CFT Triathlon Series 4 Sprint, www.sommersports.com

Adventure Kids Sprint Sr. Youth, www.adventurekids.org

Triamerica Miami Sprint, www.sommersports.com

Georgia

Lake Chatuge Challenge Sprint, www.gsmtc.com

Acworth Sprint Triathlon, www.gamultisports.com

Idaho

Palouse Sprint Triathlon, stuorgs.uidaho.edu~triclubpst_info.htm

Illinois

Wolf Creek Sprint Triathlon, www.mattoonbeachtri.com

Naperville Sprint Triathlon, www.napervilletri.com

TriAmerica Zion Sprint, www.sommersports.com

Fleet Feet Super Sprint, www.chicagotriathlon.com

Indiana

Indianapolis Sprint Triathlon, www.tuxbro.com

Optimist Triathlon Mideast Sprint Championship, www.warsawoptimist.org

Culver Fitness Centers Sprint Triathlon, www.culver.org

Iowa

Pigman Triathlon Sprint, www.pigmantri.com

Kansas

Topeka Tinman Triathlon Sprint, www.topekatinman.com

Shawnee Mission Medical Center Triathlon Sprint, www.jcprd.com

Midwest Mayhem Sprint, www.midwestmultisportraces.com

Kentucky

Shelby County Supersprint Tri, www.headfirstperformance.com

TriAmerica Louisville Sprint, www.sommersports.com

Midwest Meltdowndevil's Du Sprint, www.midwestmultisportraces.com

Scheller's Fitness & Cycling Sprint Duathlon, www.khfduathlonseries.com

Maine

Ironbear Sprint Triathlon, www.trimainiac.com/ironbear

Massachusetts

Sudbury Spring Sprint Tri, www.firmracing.com

Lions Spring Sprint Triathlon, www.firmracing.com

Hyannis Sprint Tri #1, www.timeoutproductions.com

YMCA Dual Triathlon Sprint, www.musselmantri.com

Falmouth Sprint Triathlon, www.timeoutproductions.com

Sheriff's Sprint Triathlon, www.firmracing.com

Hyannis Sprint 2 Triathlon, www.timeoutproductions.com

Michigan

Mark Mellon Memorial Triathlon Sprint, www.eliteendeavors.com

Three Rivers Triathlon Sprint, www.cooltri.com

Minnesota

Manitou Sprint Triathlon, www.manitoutri.com

Minneman Sprint, www.minnemantri.com

TriAmerica St. Paul Sprint, www.sommersports.com

Mississippi

Tri4god Sprint Triathlon, www.tri4god.com

Nevada

Pyramid Lake Sprint Triathlon, www.renoareatriathletes.com

Las Vegas Sprint Triathlon, www.lasvegastriathlon.com

New Hampshire

Timberman Triathlon Sprint, www.timbermantri.com

New Jersey

New Jersey Devilman Tri Sprint, www.piranhasports.com

Pine Barrens Sprint Triathlon, www.pinebarrenstri.org

Sunset Sprint Duathlon, www.linmark.com

New York

Sky High Sprint Offroad Triathlon, www.skyhighadventures.com

Keuka Lake Triathlon, www.keukalaketri.com

Tupper Lake Sprint Triathlon, www.tupperlakeinfo.com

A Tri in the Buff Sprint, www.scorethis.com

Musselman Triathlon Sprint, www.musselmantri.com

Montauk Point Lighthouse Sprint Triathlon, www.metrotri.com

Skaneateles Skinnyman Sprint Triathlon, www.skanraces.com

North Carolina

Cornelius Sprint Triathlon, www.setupinc.com

White Lake Sprint Triathlon, www.setupinc.com

Surf & Turf May 14 Super Sprint Tri, www.setupinc.com

Bald Head Island Sprint Tri, www.setupinc.com

Kure Beach Double Sprint Triathlon, www.setupinc.com

UNC Wellness Center Super Sprint, www.setupinc.com

Ohio

Deer Creek Duathlon Sprint, www.hfpracing.com

Maumee Bay Triathlon Sprint, www.hfpracing.com

Caesar Creek Triathlon Sprint, www.hfpracing.com

East Fork Triathlon Sprint, www.hfpracing.com

Buckeye Lake Triathlon Sprint, www.hfpracing.com

Sylvania Triathlon Sprint, www.eliteendeavors.com

Greater Cleveland Triathlon Sprint, www.trifind.netcleveland.com

Buck Creek Triathlon Sprint, www.hfpracing.com

Buck Creek Duathlon Sprint, www.hfpracing.com

Oklahoma

OKC Super Sprint Triathlon, www.okccc.edurcs.com

Oregon

Albany Sprint Triathlon, www.racecenter.com

Newport Offroad Sprint Tri Sr. Youth, www.newportswimteam.org

Newport Offroad Sprint Tri, www.newportswimteam.org

Newport Offroad Sprint Tri Jr. Youth, www.newportswimteam.org

Pennsylvania

Oxford Athletic Club Sprint Triathlon, www.runhigh.com

South Carolina

Greenwood Family YMCA Sprint Triathlon, www.gwdymca.org

Hartsville YMCA Triathlon Sprint, www.setupinc.com

Tennessee

Tellico Sprint Triathlon, www.racedayevents.net

Texas

Bobcat Sprint Triathlon, www.studentorgs.txstate.edu/triathlon

Dirty Du Rocky Hill Ranch Sprint, www.dirtyduathlon.com

Benbrook Sprint Tri, www.ironheadrp.com

Pure Austin Triathlon Sprint, www.uphillproductions.com

Metroplex Sprint Tri, www.ironheadrp.com

Power Maiden Sprint Triathlon, www.ironheadrp.com

TriAmerica Irving Sprint, www.sommersports.com

Aquarena Sprint Triathlon, www.seidelproductions.com

Splash Dash Sprint, www.trimania.com

Utah

Echo Challenge Triathlon Sprint, www.triutah.com

Cache Valley Classic Sprint, www.triutah.com

Jordanelle Triathlon Sprint, www.triutah.com

Ogden Valley Triathlon Sprint, www.triutah.com

Virginia

Angels Race Sprint Tri, www.setupinc.comangelsrace.org

Kinetic Sprint, www.setupinc.com

Virginia Run Sprint Tri, www.finswheelsfeet.com

Victory Nissan Sprint Tri, www.richmondmultisports.com

Triamerica Hampton Sprint, www.sommersports.com

Charlottesville Sprint Triathlon, www.cvilletriathlete.com

Summer Super Sprint Tri, www.triitnow.com

Washington

Mt. Rainer Sprint Du, www.buduracing.com

Righteous Richland Sprint Triathlon, www.3rrr.org

Satsop Sprint Triathlon, www.buduracing.com

Heart of the Sound Sprint Triathlon, www.heartofthesoundtriathlon.com

Wisconsin

Wisconsin Triterium Triathlon Sprint, www.triloop.org

Aurora High Cliff Triathlon Sprint, www.midwestsportsevents.com

Big Foot Triathlon Sprint, www.customcompetitions.com

Lake Michigan Triathlon Series Sprint, www.lakegenevasports.com

Pewaukee Lake Triathlon Series Super Sprint, www.lakegenevasports.com

Pleasant Prairie Triathlon Sprint, www.pleasantprairietriathlon.com

Lake Geneva Triathlon Series Super Sprint, www.lakegenevasports.com

Lake Geneva Triathlon Series Sprint, www.lakegenevasports.com

APPENDIX I: TRIATHLON RESOURCES

Triathlon Books

The following are popular and helpful books on triathlon. All are in print as of this writing.

Bernhardt, G. *Training Plans for Multisport Athletes.* Boulder, CO: VeloPress, 2000.

Carmichael, C. *Training Tips for Cyclists and Triathletes.* Boulder, CO: VeloPress, 2001.

Edwards, S. *The Complete Book of Triathlons.* Roseville, CA: Prima Publishing, 2001.

Evans, M. *Triathlete's Edge.* Champaign, IL: Human Kinetics, 2003.

Fitzgerald, M. *Complete Triathlon Book.* New York: Warner Books, 2003.

Friel, J. *The Triathlete's Training Bible.* Boulder, CO: VeloPress, 2004.

Friel, J., and G. Byrn. *Going Long: Training for Ironman-Distance Triathlons.* Boulder, CO: VeloPress, 2003.

Harr, E. *Triathlon Training in Four Hours a Week.* Emmaus, PA: Rodale Press, 2003.

Hobson, W., C. Campbell, and M. Vickers. *Swim, Bike, Run.* Champaign, IL: Human Kinetics, 2001.

Huddle, P., and R. Frey. *Triathlon: Starting Out.* Oxford, UK: Meyer & Meyer Sport, 2003.

Mora, J. *Triathlon 101.* Champaign, IL: Human Kinetics, 1999.

Niles, R. *Time-Saving Training for Multisport Athletes.* Champaign, IL: Human Kinetics, 1997.

Triathlon Web Sites

www.duathlon.com. In addition to its emphasis on duathlon, this site also provides updates on triathlon along with a race calendar, a forum, and other topics.

www.insidetri.com. This is the official Web site of *Inside Triathlon* magazine and includes race coverage, a race calendar, a forum, and more.

www.ironmanlive.com. This is the official Web site of all Ironman-sanctioned races. It provides links to the official Web sites of each Ironman qualified, training tips, live coverage of Ironman races, and more.

www.slowtwitch.com. Slowtwitch covers a broad range of topics, including race results, product reviews, training advice, and editorial comment on the goings-on in the world of triathlon.

www.trainingpeaks.com. This is an interactive Web site at which you can log your workouts online, plan your training, and analyze your performance. There is also a forum here moderated by coaches.

www.transitiontimes.com. *Transition Times* features news about triathlon, training programs, helpful information, and race coverage.

www.triathlete.com. This site includes news about the sport, commentary, and an interactive community forum.

www.triathletemag.com. The Web site for *Triathlete* magazine provides a race calendar, race results and coverage, updates on the sport of triathlon, and more.

www.triathloncentral.com. Books about triathlon and a ranking of professional triathletes along with triathlon advertising are the main features.

www.trinewbies.com. The main feature here is the moderated forum, intended primarily for those who are new to the sport. Also included is information about the sport and training programs.

www.ultrafit.com. Here you will find coaches for hire in the United States and other countries, along with a free newsletter—*e-Tips*—and a listing of camps and clinics.

www.usatriathlon.org. This is the official Web site of the USA Triathlon Federation, the governing body of the sport in the United States. It has a race calendar, information on clubs and coaches, a membership application, and updates on the sport.

www.xtri.com. This Aussie-based site focuses on long-course racing and commentary, as well as results.

www.yourfirsttri.com. The official Web site of this book; here you will find information on the training plans in Chapter 9, coaching, camps, clinics, and more.

ABOUT THE AUTHOR

JOE FRIEL HAS TRAINED endurance athletes since 1980. His clients come from all corners of the globe and include novice, elite amateur, and professional road cyclists, mountain bikers, triathletes, and duathletes, as well as national champions, world championships competitors, and an Olympian.

Joe holds a master's degree in exercise science. He is a founder and past chairman of the USA Triathlon National Coaching Commission. He is a featured columnist for *Inside Triathlon* and *VeloNews* magazines.

Joe conducts seminars around the country on training and racing for cyclists, multisport athletes, and coaches and provides consulting services for corporations in the fitness industry. He is the founder and president of Ultrafit Associates (www.ultrafit.com), Training Peaks (www.trainingpeaks.com), and Training Bible Coaching (www.trainingbible.com).

As an age-group competitor, Joe is a Colorado State Masters triathlon champion, a Rocky Mountain region and Southwest region duathlon age-group champion, and has represented the USA at the world championships several times. He enjoys competing in road-running races and USCF bike races.

Joe lives and trains on the side of the McDowell Mountains in Scottsdale, Arizona, on the edge of the Sonoran Desert. He may be reached at jfriel@trainingbible.com.